The GAME BEHIND the GAME

Mastering the Art of Bullshit

RUSS PARR

www.fgpbooks.com

Publisher: Farrah Gray Publishing
P.O. Box 33355
Las Vegas, NV 89133

Karyn Langhorne Folan
Dr. Marcia Brevard Wynn
Cover Photo ©Russ Parr

TABLE OF CONTENTS

INTRODUCTION

Meet my friend Kevondre. Yes, *Kevondre*. I'm sure his mother, Kevonna, and his daddy, Andre, knew what they were doing when they bestowed that little gem of a name on him. In the interest of complete honesty, he's not really my friend. I made him up, but I've heard stories like his before—and so have you.

Here's his situation—he's broke, needs a job or his mama is gonna kick him out, and since he's sick of her nagging, he decides to take some action. He grabs his phone, calls down to the mall, or the grocery store, or the place advertising in the local paper or online, and he says, "Yo, this Kevondre. My boys call me 'Dre Dog.' I understand that y'all got some job opportunities up in that piece and I was wonderin' if I could come down there and apply. Cool, cool? I can get down there between eleven and twelve. My boy gonna drop me off. Cool, cool."

Not cool.

Kevondre lost this one as soon as he opened his mouth. Really, he lost this one as soon as he said his *name.* See Rule Number Two of this book, cleverly entitled "Who Was Drunk When They Came Up with Your Name?" The point is, Kevondre can have his boy drop him off tomorrow if he wants; he can show up right at 11 am on the dot, and it won't matter. Even if he smells like the Old Spice guy (and not like he usually does—you know, half a bag of weed, masked with incense), he still isn't gonna get hired. When he rolls up in that store or office, instead of a job opportunity, that joint is gonna have two extra security guards posted out front. Kevondre won't be worried about those security guards, of course. He never goes anywhere without his pit. The dog hasn't had any shots and might be rabid, but as long as he stays tied up at the bicycle rack outside, that shouldn't be a problem on a job interview, right?

I know what you're thinking. You're thinking that I'm doing some racial profiling of the employment-related kind. You're thinking that nobody would actually be that stupid. You're thinking that I'm being unfair.

You'd be surprised, as I have been, over and over again when I have interviewed young Black people, who, like Kevondre, profile themselves when they make dumbass mistakes when they go out looking for work. I've had a number of young brothers and sisters come into the radio station to interview with me—and *shock* me by feeling comfortable to be as 'hood as they want to be.

Yeah, I'm Black too, but they still don't get hired—partly because I live by the rules of this book, including Rule Number Seven.

The fact is, people pre-judge each other based on the information presented. They do it all the time, and all the anti-discrimination laws in the world won't change that. I do it. Everyone does it—including you.

Yeah, *you*.

Sure, Kevondre is an extreme—he's an example of all the things these young folks do wrong rolled into one—but making even one of his mistakes is enough to get the door slammed in your face.

What did Kevondre do wrong?

As soon as he picked up the phone to call about job prospects, Kevondre presented information that told his potential supervisors that he probably wasn't going to be a good employee. When he arrived for his interview, he presented information that scared people (i.e. the rabid pit tied to a bicycle rack by the front door, smelling like weed), he used slang, and he talked about "his boy" coming by with him. All of that screamed loudly and clearly that Kevondre wasn't ready for the workplace. He presented information that predicted that he wasn't going to be "one of the good ones." In case you aren't familiar with it, "one of the good ones" is a subliminal phrase that isn't usually spoken out loud, but that doesn't mean it's not there, lurking in the back a potential employer's mind. It means that you don't fit their particular negative stereotypes about young Black folks. You might hate that people stereotype, and you might wish they didn't, but you're not in the business of trying to get them to change their stereotypes when you're trying to get hired. Your first job is to accept the fact that stereotypes exist, and then try to defeat them. You *want* to be "one of the good ones," whether your potential boss is white, Black, Latino or Asian. You *don't* want to fit anyone's stereotype, and doing that means you're probably going to have to ditch the name "Kevondre!"

What should Kevondre have done?

He should have played the game. He should have adopted the strategy of bullshit. He should have put on his best Anglo American anchorman voice, and said, "Hello, are you are accepting applications? If I come by tomorrow afternoon, would that be convenient?"

When he got there—with his brown skin and his crazy name, both of which he should assume will be strikes against him—he should have done everything he could to make the folks who worked there *like* him, trust him and feel like he was "one of the good ones."

Does it sound like I'm talking about being an "Uncle Tom?"

Update, man. I'm talking about doing what it takes to get where you need to be. You don't have to like what I'm saying, but it's the truth.

Does this sound like ass-kissing?

I will kiss an ass—especially if the only people who know there's been any ass-kissing are me and the ass kiss-ee.

Besides, "ass-kissing" is such an antiquated phrase. I prefer to think of it as game-playing that leads to cash-checking. I prefer to think of it as "strategy," and in this economy, you're going to need strategy, because in case you haven't heard, these are hard times.

The Great Recession has thrown people of all races and cultural backgrounds out of jobs, but as in so many other areas of life, Black Americans have gotten the worst of it. The national unemployment rate hovers around 9 percent, but for African Americans, the unemployment rate is 15.8 percent. If you're a Black man, it's even higher, cruising in at around 16.5 percent. If you're a Black teenage male, forget it. Almost half—44 percent--of Black men under the age of 20 are laying at Mama's house, mastering Madden and smoking a cigarette—all right, a blunt(and for the record, incense does *not* cover the smell of that stuff!)

This is no joke. Unemployment for young Black people, and for Black Americans of all ages, is extremely high. Getting a job, and keeping one, isn't a simple proposition. There are many reasons why young Blacks are unemployed and many more reasons why those that *are* employed aren't moving up as quickly as they want or need to. When I speak with young people, both on *The Russ Parr Morning Show* and when I'm asked to do events in cities across the nation, it strikes me that some of the problems come from a messed up understanding about the whole process of succeeding while Black, also known as "SWB." These young heads, and plenty of older ones, too, don't understand that job-seeking, job-keeping and job-succeeding are *games*. They're games with rules. They're games that require certain skills and certain strategies that, if you understand and take the time to practice, can have you sailing through job interviews, sailing through performance reviews, and sailing up the salary ladder of whatever endeavor or industry you choose.

It's like *World of Warcraft*, without a console. Or guns, of course. Like *World of Warcraft*, you've got to have some kind of strategy, and you've got to play to win. It can even be kind of fun.

Serious.

Yeah, I hear you grumbling. You're saying, "Yeah, Russ Parr. You talking about putting on that 'white guy' voice and doin' all that fake stuff. But I ain't gonna change myself for nobody! I'm Black and proud, baby. I'ma be *me!*"

Fine. That's your choice, but understand, sometimes in order to get what you want, "being *me*" isn't going to get you there. You can be Black and proud, but why not be Black and *paid?*

Others of you out there are thinking, "Yeah, that's fine for you, Russ Parr, with your cushy radio job and your movies and your nice life. All that stuff might work for you, but what does any of that got to do with me and my life?"

Everything, because I've been in your shoes. I want to impress you with my knowledge of bullshit and keep you listening to my radio show until I'm fired, and keep you renting my movies until I either get too broke or too tired to make 'em anymore. I have an agenda, too, you know. This ain't all about *you*, okay?

I've been working since I was a 17-year-old father with a child to help support. I've had as many as four low-waged jobs at one time—and gone to school, too. I've been so broke that I wasn't exactly starving, but a Happy Meal was a luxury. I've struggled and gone without sleep—and even broken the law—just to survive. Yes, my father could have given me money on a number of occasions, and he did on quite a few, but I didn't want to ask for his help because I knew it came with strings attached. He did that on purpose. He made it hard for me to ask, so hard that I did it only when I was truly desperate. I see now the lesson he was teaching me, but at the time, it sometimes felt like he was leaving me twisting in the wind. Now that I'm a father to teen-aged sons, I know that it devastated my father to have to take that approach with me. In hindsight, I'm so glad he did. Otherwise I might be out there somewhere holding up tollbooths for quarters, or selling oregano.

I know what it feels like to be unemployed, be underemployed, and to be working poor. I also know what it feels like to be working for people who didn't want to hire me because I was Black. I know what it feels like to be working for people who wanted to fire me because I was Black. I know what it feels like to be working with people who hired me and then *expected* to fire me because I was Black. I know what it feels like to not get promotions because I was Black, too. I know what it's like to work with Black people who wanted to see me become unemployed—and who did everything they could to make that happen because I was Black, too. Okay, okay I'll calm down on the "because I'm Black" thing, but you get my point. Working while Black isn't the easiest thing in the world to do—even when you work mainly around other Black people, people.

From these employers, co-workers and situations, and from my parents who gave me my first lessons on the game behind the game, I learned the strategies for success that I'm going to teach you in this book. Succeeding while Black is an art, but it's one that you can perfect if you're willing to set aside your own preconceptions, learn the rules I will outline in the next fourteen chapters, and practice them in your own quest to master the game behind the game.

Now, I know some of the rules of this game might make you a little a nervous. Actually I don't give a f^% if they do! I'm going to tell you some things that may seem contrary to what you would normally do—that's why I call myself "The Opposite Guy" or "The Non-Conformist," but I promise that doing the opposite of what people expect is a powerful strategy in perfecting the art of bullshit. If you learn to play the opposite, along with other rules in this book, you'll be well on your way to cash-checking and to helping me sell more books—then I'll be able to write another book and make more movies. That will help my bottom line immensely—and yours, too!

If you're out of a job, this book is for you.

If you're looking for a better job, this book is for you.

If you're looking to start a new career, this book is for you.

If you're looking to take your old career to a new level, this book is for you.

If you're looking to get your grown-ass child out of your basement, this book is for you.

If you're looking for the story of just how I've made the career I've made, this book is for you.

The only people who shouldn't read this book are my current bosses and anyone I owe money to.

For the rest of you, read and enjoy my book, because I'm sure I will when I get around to reading it.

Happy cash-checking!

RULE #1:

A Little Bit of Bullshit Goes a Long Way

Most people already think they know about talking bullshit. They even think of "bullshitting" as a bad thing.

Well, let me hip you to something vitally important, people:

Bullshit runs the world! You can dress it up and call it whatever you want, but at the end of the day it's *all* bullshit. Those who understand this simple truth and learn how to play the game go places in life. Those that don't understand it don't fare as well.

My good friend, actor and comedian Kevin Hart, understands this all too well. He has bullshitted his way to being the best in his craft. He's small, funny-looking and was never expected to make it to where he is now, but he realized at a young age that he could make fun of himself. He's been able to parlay that ability into an extremely successful entertainment career. His comedy DVDs have sold into the millions, and he's been in several movies (including a couple of mine.) He's slated to play a flying monkey in the remake of *The Wizard of Oz*. Seriously, he's the *lead* monkey, in case you rent the film.

How did a short, funny-looking dude like him make it to *lead monkey*?

Kevin knew how to bullshit, he knew how to make people like him and he knew how to combine those abilities in a way that made people want to help him achieve his goals. Yes, he's endured plenty of short jokes, and now he's enduring "flying monkey" jokes, but he doesn't get offended (because he isn't). Even if he were offended, he'd never let on. He's playing the game behind the game. He's been playing it from the beginning to get where he needed to be. He is a master of Bullshit-ology—just like me.

What do I mean by "bullshit?"

"Bullshit" is the art of persuasion. It's the ability to pontificate wildly imaginative fantastical versions of reality and get others to invest in them willingly and enthusiastically. Bullshit is theatrical: it's a cousin of acting. It's historical: it's been handed down through the centuries from Black parents to their children. It's literary: Paul Lawrence Dunbar wrote about it in his famous poem "We Wear the Mask." And it's absolutely necessary if you want to get something better than what you've got.

Bullshit is the ability to embellish, without totally lying. It's the ability to manipulate, without being mean-spirited. It's the ability to sell people your version of who you are, what you've done and what they're going to do to help you get to where you want to be next. It's really hard to hate or expose a truly talented bullshitter.

It's not a stretch for my friend, Kevin Hart, to sell people on the idea that he'd make an incredible flying monkey, even though he's never taken on such a demanding role. When I was casting my first movie, *The Last Stand,* Kevin came in and said he wanted to do the lead. I'd already cast Guy Torry in that role, but Kevin was persistent. "Watch this, watch this!" he kept saying. Then he did a performance of the lead role that was just amazing.

I loved his performance, but being a man of my word, I couldn't recast. Guy had been really good, too, and I'd already given him the part, but Kevin's performance impressed the hell out of me. Since I was the writer, producer and director of the film, I had an idea.

"Give me 15 minutes," I told Kevin. I ran upstairs and wrote in two new characters, G-SPOT and F-STOP. Kevin would play a bad ventriloquist with a dummy that looked like him, that Kevin's character believed was a real person. I wrote in a very dramatic scene where Kevin's character unraveled mentally and emotionally on stage. Kevin had everyone in tears when he played it.

I hear you saying, "Okay, what's your point?"

Kevin proved to me at that audition that he wasn't just a one trick pony. He proved he was more than just a comedic actor. Kevin sold me on someone I thought didn't exist—Kevin Hart, dramatic actor. Now *that* was some bullshit. By the way, I was kidding about the flying monkey role. That doesn't exist at all, but you believed me, didn't you? See, bullshit in action!

If I weren't fluent in BS, I would have never gotten my

BA. If it weren't for BS, I wouldn't be where I am today, and I'm not the only one. The ability to bullshit is one of the cornerstones of succeeding while Black (SWB),and anyone who says otherwise is bullshitting. If it weren't for his ability to bullshit, Barack Obama would never have become President of the United States. Think about *that*!

BS'ing a BA.

I've known for a long time that I could make people believe that I knew what I was talking about, even when I didn't.

When I was in college at Cal-State Northridge, I had a professor named Dr. Donald Woods. The guy was formidable—that means scary, for those of you still reading at the Dr. Seuss level—because he was head of the department of Radio, Television and Film. He'd been there for years and I'm sure he'd heard all kinds of bullshit in his tenure at the University, some of it creative, most not. I'm sure it wasn't his intention to be intimidating, but he was such a deep thinker and intellectual that it was really hard to get a decent grade out of his classes. Most of us were pretty scared of him because of that.

At this time in my life, I was a young father, working night and day trying to support my son. I probably had three or four jobs and was mostly worried about keeping food on the table. I was enrolled in school because I knew I needed a degree to make more money. Of course, plenty of people have made tons of money *without* a degree, but since I wasn't sure I would be one of them, I went to school.

I was in school, but I didn't spend much time on my class work. I was working so much that there wasn't a whole lot of time for assignments. I was literally working around the clock, just trying to afford a Happy Meal, but I managed to get to my classes, usually tired as hell. I'd sit in the back and hope not to be noticed, but one day, Dr. Woods called on me.

I hadn't read the material, but I didn't let that fact stop me. My mother was a school teacher and she'd often told me how important it was to always contribute something verbally in the classroom, even if you had no understanding of the topic at hand. According to her, just trying to say something intelligent gave you brownie points. "You might have missed the point and gotten it all wrong, but the instructor will think you're interested. That's a good thing!"

Mom knew all about bullshit.

"Mr. Parr," Dr. Woods began, in his intimidating professorial voice. "What do you think about the questions on page 134?"

I had no idea what he was talking about. I hadn't read the questions on page 134 and I certainly didn't have any thoughts on them, but I quickly flipped to the page, scanned it and started talking, reaching for whatever knowledge I had. I spun out some completely made-up answer and I kept talking like I knew something, until Dr. Woods stopped me.

"How many of you agree with Mr. Parr's assessment?" he asked the room.

Hands shot up all around me. What I said sounded good, and most of my fellow students hadn't read any more of the assignment than I had.

Dr. Woods chuckled. "Ladies and gentlemen, not a word of what Mr. Parr has just said is correct. None of it. He's bullshitted you all and you fell for every syllable. Everybody will receive an F and Mr. Parr will receive a B."

I was stunned, and so was the rest of the class. I'm sure I wasn't very popular that day. As the rest of the students filed out of the room, I crept up to the front of the room and asked him, "Why did you give me a B?"

"Because you participated," he replied, but after that, he was on to me. I was always the first one to raise my hand, but he ignored me unless he wanted some comic relief. He might not have let me say much in class, but Dr. Woods took a liking to me from that day forward and I know it was partly because I was such a confident bullshitter. He knew that the ability to produce competent bullshit on cue is an immensely valuable skill in this world, and my raw sewage—I mean raw *talent*—impressed him. Because I had invested in developing that ability, he decided to invest his expertise in me (I'll talk more about investing in your talents in Rule Number Six). Throughout my college career, Dr. Woods helped and guided me, all because of a little bullshit I spouted one day in his classroom.

I tell this story because it makes one critical point that every young person should know: Looking and sounding like you know what you're talking about is sometimes just as important as *actually* knowing what you're talking about. Being able to persuade people, whether it's in an interview, in a presentation or in a contest for political office, is one of the most important skills you'll ever need.

SOME AUTOBIOGRAPHICAL BS

I learned to BS because, as a child, I was in a difficult position. Making friends was complicated for me, thanks to the education, economics and the class/caste system of the United States Air Force.

I was a military brat. We moved a lot, which always posed a problem when it came to making and keeping friends. We lived in Holyoke, Massachusetts, we lived in Guam, we lived in Texas—where I was born—and we lived in California. Moving around made friendships harder, but moving was only part of the problem. The other part of the problem was that my father was an officer—one of the few Black officers at that time.

It was the 1960s, a decade that was full of social upheaval and change as the Civil Rights movement forced integration into institutions across the country. As those of you who have either read or lived through some history know, the military had been integrated since 1948, but that didn't mean everything was roses for Black men in the military. Most of the Black officers in the Air Force weren't promoted above the rank of Captain, and Captain isn't a particularly high rank. My father was skilled at playing the game, and although he used his own ways of bullshitting his superior officers, even he wasn't immune to the racism that still pervaded the Air Force's officer corps. More on what his experiences taught me about playing the game behind the game later. As a kid,however, his rank presented a problem for me because most of the Black soldiers—and their families—were enlisted, not officers.

The military separates officers from enlisted men. Officers have separate housing with other officers. They have their own hang outs, separate from enlisted men. This goes back for centuries with military units—as far back as the Roman Empire, I think—based on the idea that it's not good for the men in command to get too close to the regular foot soldiers, who are probably going to get killed anyway. "Fraternization" is the word they use for it, and it's frowned upon.

So, if you were an officer's kid, you lived in one neighborhood; if your father was enlisted, you lived somewhere else. If you were an officer's kid, you might have a pool pass to one pool, and a different one if you were an enlisted soldier's kid. I actually swam and peed in both pools, but you get the picture. We all went to the same schools, but we didn't all have the same life when we left there.

My sister, my brother and I were isolated from everyone else a lot of the time. The Black kids on base, most of whom had enlisted parents, didn't have what we had financially. As an officer, our father made more money—a whole $25,000! It was a lot of money in the 1960s, and because of it, they assumed that we were stuck up. They were suspicious of us. Most of the other officers' kids were white and those kids were suspicious of us, too, because we were Black.

Since we only had each other, we ended up coming up with ways to entertain ourselves. We had shows in the basement of our house. That's where I first started to fool around with characters and voices and stuff. I learned to be funny to entertain myself, then I discovered that being funny amused other people, too. I used the bullshit I developed at home to neutralize the pre-conception that some kids had of me—that I was either an elitist snob because my dad was an officer, or an angry militant because I was Black—and to create a different perception of me altogether, Russ Parr "funny guy." They had no idea I really *was* an angry, Black, elitist, snob!

The point is, my efforts to make my peers laugh was complete bullshit, but it was fun—and funny—and it seemed to work.

Humor for me is just natural. I grew up in a house full of comedians. My older brother, Rodney, was very funny—and still is—he just doesn't know it. My mother, Betty, was witty—the sort of person who had a tremendous vocabulary and could twist words and make something hilarious out of them. My dad, Thomas, is more the sarcastic type with biting, cutting humor. My sister, Cheryl, was my audience. She always laughed at stuff I would do and say, and still does to this very day—only these days, she needs at least two glasses of wine to make me feel like I'm still funny. See, she bullshits, too. So many of the roles and characters I've created came from my childhood, but when I used them outside of our house, I had an agenda. Then, it was to make friends, to be popular and to get people to do what I wanted them to do. Now, it's to make money, get ratings and get people to do what I want them to do.

I got better and better at spouting bullshit and getting what I wanted as I grew older. By the time I was in high school, I was pretty good at it. By the time I met Dr. Donald Woods at Cal-State Northridge, I was a master.

HOW TO MAKE YOUR BULLSHIT WORK FOR YOU

I'm always amazed how many young Black people don't realize that they need to use their bullshit to sell themselves into employment! It's not that they don't *know* how to bullshit—they do. It's just that they use it on the wrong people. They'd rather bullshit their homies. I say, "Apply that art on the job! Don't waste it on Stevon because you know he's coming back to whup your ass for selling him a bag of oregano. Yeah, you bullshitted him into buying some seasoning, but to me, that's a waste of talent. Aim higher!"

In reality, a job interview is the best place to perfect the fine art of bullshit. Actually, you should practice *before* the interview so that you have your strategies in mind. You should know how you're going to answer certain questions, have your stories together about any . . . uh, *gaps* . . . in your employment history or weaknesses in your employment experiences. The semi-honesty of bullshit is appropriate here. There's information you should volunteer ("I'm especially good at counting and accounting for money") and information you shouldn't

("That two-year gap on my resume is from the time I was locked up for embezzling.") You should know how much to embellish your resume—and how much is too far to be believable—and most important, you should know what *not* to say and do in an interview (like trying to sell your potential employer a bag of oregano!)

Now, here's a lesson in bullshitting your way into a job, from a "master."

While I was in my last year of college, I applied for a job at ABC-TV. Well, not exactly. I *wanted* a job at ABC-TV, but I knew that sending in an application wouldn't get me very far. It was very difficult to get a job at a major television network then. It still is. There were long waiting lists for every kind of job imaginable at ABC, and I was pretty sure that if I just sent in a resume, it would quickly get filed away and never be seen again. So I concocted a plan—a bullshit plan that I thought would at least get me in front of the HR director.

I called ABC-TV. "Hello, my name is Russell Parr and I'm a student at Cal-State Northridge in the Radio, Television and Film program," I said in my most polite and obsequious voice. (Look it up, I'm not your dictionary . . . and don't name your daughter Obsequious, please!)

"I have to do a paper for school about how hiring procedures in television differ from other media. Do you think I could get an interview with the HR Director?"

This was a total and complete lie. There was no paper. It was simply a strategy to get some face-time with the HR Director. I hoped that if the guy knew my name and remembered me, when I applied for a job it might help me stand out from the pack of resumes on his desk.

I spoke with one of his assistants and gave her this whole song and dance about my paper, my due dates and so forth. Some of it I had prepared and some I just tapped dance around, but it must have been some pretty convincing bullshit because within a week, they called me in for this "interview" with the HR Director for my "project."

I wrote down a list of fake questions and headed off to meet him, feeling pretty proud of myself. I was master of bullshit! I was the man! But in the middle of my fake questions, the HR guy stopped me.

"Mr. Parr, do you really have to write a paper for a school project?" he asked.

"Yes sir," I began. I had intended to play out my bullshit role until the bitter end. Then I saw the look on his face.

He was on to me. Keeping up the façade wouldn't accomplish my intended goal. That's the thing about bullshit. There's such a thing as going too far, and once you do, you have to acknowledge it and cut your losses. One look at that man's face, and I knew it was time to tell the truth.

"Ah, no sir. There's no paper."

"You came down here to get a job, didn't you?"

I hesitated.

"Yes," I admitted, and quickly apologized to him for the deception. I explained how eager I was to work for ABC and that I really just hoped to learn more about what the network was looking for in its hiring procedures.

"Well, Mr. Parr, you're going to need a resume," he said. I reached for my bag. He said, "Let me guess. You have a resume right in there."

I apologized again. "Yes, I do, sir."

He sat back in his chair and stared at me what seem like for ten minutes. I could feel the sweat on my forehead and my back. I wasn't sure if I'd done something criminal or not, but I was pretty sure I was about to get kicked out of this man's office. I started worrying that he'd call Cal-State Northridge and I'd be formally disciplined. Would they keep me from graduating next semester? Would all the suffering and sacrifices I'd made to get my degree be worthless because of this crazy idea to bullshit far above my level?

I was scared to death.

Then the guy started laughing. "This is a first for me. Anyone willing to jump through these hoops just to get a job here is not just your average applicant. I'm going to find you something, Mr. Parr."

My bullshit worked, but I was sweating bullets. I really didn't know whether the guy would find my strategy creative and amusing, or if he'd call security! And while I wouldn't recommend taking BS to the level I did in that instance, you should know what I didn't—many recruiters and job placement counselors will recommend a strategy similar to mine to get a foot in the door. They call it asking for "an informational interview." It's far less deceptive than what I did since you admit that you're asking questions about the job prospects at the office, but it's still a chance to get your foot in the door. It's a chance to bullshit your way into a real job opportunity if you do it smart.

If you've never tried something like that, and you don't have a job or you don't have the job you want, you should consider it strongly. Do some research, make some calls, write down some questions and take a resume, just in case. Sometimes, just sending in an application isn't enough. Just don't bring one of your boys or tie your pit-bull to a bicycle rack out front.

Thanks to my bullshit "paper strategy" in 1978, I had my first real, decent-paying job in radio and television, the field in which I would ultimately make my career. The HR Director at ABC-TV found me a job as Production Services Director for shows like *Welcome Back, Kotter* and *Fish,* which sounds like a really cool job. The truth was, I was paper-pusher. I was keeping track of things like how many nails were used in set construction. I filled out requisition orders. I counted light bulbs.

When it came time to look for another job and my resume said that I had been "Production Services Director" with these very popular television shows, people said, "Wow." I didn't tell them that I had been counting nails and trying to get Todd Bridges (then a nine year old child actor on *Fish*) to come down from the rafters to do his scenes.

Instead, I bullshitted. I embellished a bit on my job responsibilities, including things that I knew how to do, but weren't actually responsibilities on that job, and things that I hoped I'd someday get the chance to do. I didn't exactly lie, but I didn't correct the impression conveyed by my title, either. Bullshit begets bullshit.

It's a game, remember? It's a game, and bullshit is a significant part of that game. Take what you know about talking trash in other scenarios—in relationships, on the basketball court, whatever—and use it to get yourself in the door and up the corporate ladder.

BULLSHIT BY OMISSION

I wasn't Production Services Director for very long. Soon it was time to try for another job, and I knew which one I wanted. I wanted a job with KABC radio, but had to talk my way into that interview, too, since my resume seemed to suggest that I was headed for a TV production career. Once I got that interview, there was more bullshitting to do. This time, I was bullshitting by omission, because what I *didn't* do was tell the potential employer that I was on the brink of being fired.

Yes, *fired.*

Why? Quite a few reasons, but the biggest one was that succeeding while Black can make you enemies. My White bosses hadn't wanted to hire me, but affirmative action was mandated for almost all employers then, and was certainly in effect at ABC-TV. They had to have some Black faces in their shop, and mine fit the bill, but that didn't mean they were happy to have me, or that they wanted to see me build a career there with them. I tried to avoid irritating them—I didn't ask them to introduce me to their daughters-- but it didn't matter. They concocted a plan to document all my mistakes, without telling me that I was making the mistakes. At my six month review, they presented me with a file as thick as a couple of phone books, full of my errors. It looked like I was the biggest screw-up ever hired at ABC-TV.

It wasn't true, and it wasn't fair. If my mistakes had been pointed out to me while I was making them, I would have known what I was doing wrong and corrected it. Since no one ever told me I was screwing up, I kept making the same mistakes over and over and over.

I was young and relatively naïve, but I'd made a few people love me there at ABC-TV (That's Rule Number Three—"Make People Love You"), including an older

Jewish guy who worked in another department.

"You got to go to HR, Russ. You got to go to HR and tell 'em they set you up."

On the advice of this older man who had much more workplace experience than I did, I went back to the HR Director who had hired me. I explained that I was being railroaded and the HR guy (I remember him as a very savvy Latino guy) knew that the whole mess had the kind of racial overtones that would be bad for business. He knew ABC-TV didn't want or need a big discrimination controversy starring Russ Parr. They didn't want a big EEO lawsuit, starring Russ Parr, either. I never planned to do either one of those things. To be honest, I don't think I even *knew* I could have done those things, until years later. The HR Director knew I had those rights, so he was very eager to help me get a new position that was to my liking. If anyone had called to check on my responsibilities as a Production Services Director, I don't think HR was going to correct any bullshit I spouted with the truth of how many stacks of lumber I ordered or how many cans of paint I could count. I think they would have said, "Yes, he certainly did!" just to keep me from filing suit for discrimination.

Being the good bullshitter that I was, I used the fears of the HR department to take calculated risks in my next interviews. Yes, *calculated*, as in *math*. I calculated how far I thought I could go without getting caught, and I said just that much and no more.

It would be silly for me to go on a job interview and try to make it sound like, after less than a year as a Production Services Director, I had learned enough to be qualified to run the entire Production Office, or the Accounting Office—or even all of ABC-TV! But given that my next position was with ABC-Radio as an audio engineer, it was a reasonable gamble to embellish my responsibilities a little and to omit, entirely, the whole discussion about how my racist, and soon-to-be-former, bosses had tried to screw me. (Did I tell you I counted screws, too?)

I got the job with ABC Radio, and the rest, as they say, is history. The moral of the story is—You don't have to tell an employer everything. Sometimes the smartest way to bullshit is to just skip the messy parts and focus on the positives, like what you have to offer them that will make their lives easier and wealthier. After all, job interviews are not about *you.* Job interviews are about what you can do for *them*—and make it sound good! (This is some two hit oregano, maaan!! Okay no more weed references, but catch the point. If you're going to sell bullshit, *sell* it!)

I'm also amazed at how many people don't know that the *last* thing you want to do in a job-seeking situation is bash your old boss.

Interviewer: "Sheniquanay, why are you leaving your current employment?"

Sheniquanay: "Me and my supervisor been getting into it because she don't know what she's doing. So yesterday I just cussed her out and I'm done wid it."

Interviewer: "Next!"

Now, no one is *that* stupid, right?

Wrong.

I had a sister come in to interview with me and just because I was Black, she felt comfortable enough to actually say something pretty close to that in her interview. I guess she felt like we had some "secret alliance" because we were both Black, but that's a mistaken assumption (See Rule Number Four, where I'll break it down.) She didn't seem to realize that she was telling me she's the sort of employee who gets mad and cusses people out. At some point, I knew she would get mad and cuss *me* out—Black or not. If you enjoy getting cussed out, hire Sheniquanay.

Since I don't enjoy getting cussed out, I didn't hire her.

Sheniquanay (not her real name, of course, but you get the picture) should be playing the game, and using her words to create a different picture of the same event. If she learns to perfect her bullshit, she could say, "I feel that I'm ready for more supervisory responsibilities and there's no room for advancement where I am now. I'd like to bring everything I've learned about managing other employees to this opportunity."

Or she could just say, "I'm hoping for a position with more leadership opportunities."

It's not a lie, but it isn't the whole truth either. It's not the whole story, but it's a version of the story with some basis in reality. It has a bit of deception to it, since it conceals some of the gritty aspects of why Sheniquanay needs a new job, but the deception could fairly be called Sheniquanay's best spin on what really happened. The last thing Sheniquanay wants to do is leave the interviewer wondering if Sheniquanay's going to cuss her out before the end of the interview.

Of course, Sheniquanay shouldn't be cussing her boss out at all. The world is small, man. You never know who you're going to need in this world. Burning bridges is dangerous and stupid. There are better ways to handle idiot bosses, trust me. We'll talk about those in other rules of the game. But since she's already done it, the least she can do is not brag about it in her interview for a new job!

At this point you're saying, "Russ, you're so down on our people! You must be some sort of sell out." Let me say for the record (CD? MP3?) that I love my people. That's why I'm hitting you with this bullshit! I've seen too many talented people screw themselves out of opportunities, all because they chose to not conform to the requisite procedures for getting paid! So hate me if you want, but this bullshit *works*.

Keep reading.

KEEP YOUR STORIES STRAIGHT —OR ELSE

As I've said, a good bullshitter will brag about what he knows how to do. A good bullshitter isn't afraid to stretch the truth, but only a little. If you're going to go out on a limb and stretch the truth until it breaks into two pieces in your hands, you'd better be prepared to take a crash course in learning how to do what you've said you can do.

Say, for example, I'm in a job interview and the interviewer asks, "Have you ever done (insert your job skill here)?"

"Oh sure, I've done that," I say confidently, when the truth is, I don't even know how to spell it. "No problem!"

And I get hired.

Now, of course, I don't *actually* know how to do what they've asked, but I scramble to learn, and I ask a lot of questions of the people who do. I say, "Oh well, we did it differently at my other job!" when they question me because I'm not doing it right. Then, if I actually get called on the carpet for it, I say, "Oh, well you actually asked me if I knew how to do *Y* which I *do* know how to do. But see here, you've got me doing *Z* which is closely related, but not really the same thing. So that's why I'm having a little trouble getting it done!"

Then, I hurry up and learn how to do Z as fast as humanly possible, so my ignorance is no longer an issue. Bullshit is only good up to a point. After that, you have to perform, and that's why Rule Number Five is all about that little thing called "working hard."

Before we move into other rules, this example brings up another critical point in perfecting the art of bullshit—

If you're going to be a master bullshitter, you've got to *remember* your bullshit.

This is where a lot of wannabe bullshitters get all messed up. They just go over the top and say a lot of crazy stuff that's too obvious. Or they say something just outrageous enough that someone decides to check it out. Then they get caught. If you get caught, you're in the bad situation of having to compound your bullshit. And by compounding your bullshit, I mean that now, you've got to bullshit about your bullshit—or embellish your embellishments—and if you don't get that right, you're fired.

Here it is in its simplest form: Never say some bullshit that can be verified.

There was this dude who wanted to do some business with me. He was spinning his bullshit about how we could make movies and blah blah blah. Then he said that a lot of "money people" he knew had seen the trailer of my latest movie. He said he thought he could get me a good distribution deal.

"Did you like the trailer?" I asked him. "Did you think it was good?"

"I loved it!" he said enthusiastically.

One problem for my man, right there: I hadn't *produced* a trailer for that movie. Busted.

So he was a wrap. With the Internet, verification of most bullshit can be obtained in seconds. Do your homework before you say something that can be checked out.

Trust me, I know what I'm talking about. I've overdone it on a few occasions and I'm telling you, once you're caught, you better be ready to move on to your next "opportunity." Ideally, you'd better have that next opportunity in your hand *before* you get caught. The idea is to move on and up before anyone gets wise to what you're up to.

Working in radio like I do, I've had some practice with getting caught on some bullshit and having to create new bullshit, just to keep from getting fired. For me, this kind of difficulty usually arises when my bosses decide to listen to me on the air during my radio show. Can you imagine that? My radio bosses occasionally *listen* to my show instead of sitting in their offices doing whatever it is they're supposed to be doing! When they listen, they might occasionally hear me running them down to the listeners. Not by name of course—I'm not stupid—but they know who I'm talking about. Bam! As soon as I get done with the show, they're standing there waiting for me.

Busted.

"Russ, did you mean what you said on the air? I thought we were cool," they'd say, looking all hurt and upset. I could tell they were putting it altogether, and thinking, "Wow, Russ is really a con-artist if he could actually smile in my face while he thinks of me that way."

Now it's time for "compound bullshit" or embellished embellishments. Of course I meant what I said on the air, and of course all that "we cool" stuff was little more than me playing my game to make sure that I was loved by those I needed to be loved by. But they can't know that! It's time to do the Savion Glover, folks. Time to tap dance.

That probably sounds really cold, but in the professional sphere, "friendship" must be defined carefully. This isn't a bad thing, really. It's just the truth. No matter how pleasant the environment, at work everyone's trying to get ahead. Everyone's trying to get further up the ladder. Everyone's check-cashing. So even while you're being pleasant and friendly, there should always be a part of you that hangs back. There should always be a part of your brain that's working, playing the angles, and trying to anticipate the next move. There should always be a part of you that's figuring out what the other guy's agenda is and how to manipulate it. More on that in Rule Number

Five, but for now the lesson is simply that if you're gonna bullshit your boss, you really shouldn't be bragging about it on the radio or anywhere else.

I always play the game, but I've learned to be a lot more careful—and less obvious—in the way I weave my webs and what I say on the air about the people around me. That also gives me credibility when I tell you, it's a subtle game. Keep your BS straight, and keep a tight hold on your strategies. Be all about your bullshit, but don't go writing books about it. No need to advertise.

If you're getting busted on your bullshit (because you're BS-ing about things that can be verified, or you're going overboard and over-fertilizing), then you're not doing it right. Hit the brakes, bitch! Take baby steps! Bullshit is smart. Bullshit is calculated. Bullshit is calm. Bullshit learns from being busted. Practice makes perfected bullshit.

Bullshit can get your foot in the door. Bullshit can also get you out of a tight spot. Once, I was on an elevator with a very famous actor who shall remain anonymous. He was known for doing a *lot* of ladies, but on this elevator this particular day, he was with this really random-looking lady. I was thinking, "Where did he find *that* hooker?" when they got off ahead of me.

Well, the next morning I saw him in the lobby. "Man," I said to him. "Where did you pick up that *thing* you were with last night? I hope she paid *you*!"

He looked at me, all serious. "That was my *wife*, man."

I immediately went into defcon bullshit mode. Emergency, emergency! "I knew that was your wife, man," I said. "I was just fucking with you!" We both started laughing and everything was cool.

Whew . . .

Bullshit saves the day once again.

Seriously, you'll need a bit more than simple bullshit to move up the ladder in the workplace and in the real world. You'll need to be able to use your bullshit to make people love you—that's Rule Number Three—and you'll need to work hard—that's Rule Number Five. You might also need to change a few critical things about how you present yourself in this world, starting with your name, which is Rule Number Two.

RULE #2:

Who Was Drunk When They Came Up With Your Name?

You wouldn't believe some of the calls we get on *The Russ Parr Morning Show*. Not just the things people say, but the names of the people who call in. We've had people call in who are named after sexually transmitted diseases. We get people who are named after alcoholic beverages.

They're named after cars. They're named after the latest ghetto fabulous brand or object. Their names are the unholy union of two syllables from Mama's name and two syllables from Daddy's name.

It's funny, until you try to start a career with a name that sounds like dipthong and an independent clause got drunk, had sex and gave birth to a simile.

Yeah, I know what you're saying. I've heard it before.

"But Russ, I don't want my child to have some name that everybody else has. I want my daughter to be unique, and that's why her name is 'Uniqua.'"

"I don't want to name my child some standard Anglo American name. You're asking us to lose our Black individualism. You're asking us to sacrifice something that sets us apart from others."

Yeah, these names set us apart and make us unique, but not in a good way, I'm sorry to tell you. These are the names that put us in the unemployment lines. These are the names that have us under-achieving financially. These are the names that shut the doors on our children's future opportunities. These are the names that have marginalized our children's success. These names make them easily identifiable in a pile of resumes, and get them immediately sent to the bottom of that pile.

It's tragic when I pick up the newspaper to read about a shooting and the suspects names are Rayquan Johnson, Chevail Smith and JaVonn Lemon. I know they're all Black, you know they're all Black, and so does everyone else who reads or hears those names on the news. The names send the message, no visuals needed. The names create and embrace a negative stereotype that, unfortunately, young Black people live up to daily.

So what do you do if your Mama named you "Akbanika" and you want to be "one of the good ones?"

You do what Hollywood celebrities do, and have been doing since the first silent films. You create a new name for yourself that sells you to mass audiences. There's no shame in it. You're just going to give yourself a nickname that's less obviously black. You're giving yourself an AKA ("also known as" or an alias) specifically for the purposes of cash-checking. If "Nika" is still too obvious, come up with something else. Become "Anna" or "Bob." Create something that's close to your name, or not. It doesn't matter what it is, as long as a person reading your resume can't tell what race you are based on your name.

It's no secret why some Hollywood stars changed their names. Many of them had Jewish or other ethnic-sounding birth names. They knew the names they were born with might make it harder for them to succeed in their industry of choice. They thought their birth names might be a hindrance that might keep them from getting the more desirable roles or opportunities. So, rather than complain that the industry was "unfair" and "keeping a Jew down," they accepted the realities of the situation and changed what they could change. "Cary Grant" sounds more like a heart-throb name than "Archie Leach," right?

It worked for him in the golden age of film, and it will work for you now in your quest to be cash-checking. Changing your name won't make you less black, but it might get your foot in the door. Once your foot is in the door, you can work the rules of the game to make it easier for the next guy or girl with an ethnic sounding name.

Sorry folks, but that's how you play the game. You change what you can change, including yourself. I don't like it any more than you do, but a name like "Akbanika" creates a certain image in people's minds, and that image is likely to be negative. It's likely to be an image that will make it harder, not easier, to get what you want or dream of out of life. It's not fair, but there it is. You might be super talented, hard-working and good to people of all backgrounds and creeds, but if your name suggests something different, the chances are good that the name will shut down opportunities before people ever give you the chance to show them how great you are. The name "Akbanika" will exclude you from the chance to prove yourself, and you might never even know why you're not moving up the ladder as fast as you should or why you can't even get your foot in the door.

How can you tell if you might need to apply this rule? If you didn't learn how to spell your name correctly until you were in the fourth grade, you're a candidate. If you've read your name in the newspaper or heard it on the news associated with a criminal offense, you're a candidate. If you have the same name as one of the characters in a 'hood movie, you're a candidate.

Now, maybe if you're a truly exceptional human being, your name won't matter. Maybe it won't keep you from moving up in the world. Maybe those in power will overlook what it suggests or embrace it in all its ethnic glory, but before you put yourself in that category, think of this: even Barack Obama went by the name "Barry" for most of his life, anglicizing his birth name to make those around him more comfortable. I would consider him a pretty exceptional guy, but even he realized that he might not get the chance to show people how exceptional he was if his name stood in the way. To this day, his name is causing him problems with a certain group of truly ignorant folks. They're scared that he's a Muslim (without knowing anything about Islam.) They're scared he's not really "an 'Merican" (without being able to spell it) and so on. You get my point.

You don't have to like it, but you do have to face it. If you're gonna succeed while Black, you gotta do what you gotta do. It's a rule in the game behind the game.

RULE #3:

Make People Love You

(But Make Sure You Use Protection)

It's not hard to make people love you. You have to be able to stroke people's egos, and to do that, all you really need to do is find out what they're proud of. Find out what they love, and then admire them and it. Bullshit compliments are usually the order of the day when you need to make people love you. I can't tell you how many bosses I've told that they have a good-looking family.

You know what I'm talking about. There's a family portrait on their desk—he's smiling from ear to ear, the wife resembles a sea slug and the kids look like land lizards. "What a lovely family you have!" I exclaim.

Yes, it's a bit disingenuous (Look it up!), but those simple words will score you a ton of points on the "making people love you scale." Why? Because the family portrait, prominently displayed, tells you that your boss is a person who loves and values his family—whatever they look like. Being perceptive enough to admire them is a quick and easy way to connect to your boss over something he or she loves. It's easier for the boss to love you when have the sense to love what he loves!

As I said, admiring the boss's family is quick and easy. On occasion, though, you'll have a harder time connecting to your superiors because you come from very different worlds. Maybe you come from different parts of the country or different religious backgrounds. You might be of different races or have completely different points of view on everything from sports to music to politics. On the surface, it might seem like you have nothing at all in common, but I'm telling you, if you're going to be cash-checking—if you're going to learn to play the game behind the game—it's your job to find some way to *make* that boss love you.

I know what I'm talking about, because one of my very first bosses was a redneck.

I don't mean a DLR—a down low redneck. You know them, right? Those are the guys who wear suits and ties and you can't actually tell that their necks are red underneath there until they say or do something so obviously racist that there's no longer any doubt.

No, I mean an actual tobacco-spitting, NASCAR-watching, whiskey-drinking, Confederate-flag waving redneck. Or at least that's what I would have called him before I got to know him as a person. This was back in the late 70's and he was my manager at an auto parts store that will remain nameless. I was a struggling college student, and working with him was just one of my many jobs. I knew he didn't like me. He saw me through the same narrow lens that made me categorize him as a "redneck," and he was suspicious of me because I was a Black man. I knew that unless I could find a way to connect to him as a *person*—reaching beyond the black and white of the situation—I wouldn't be working there long.

I was probably about 19 and I needed the money from

that job badly. My oldest son, Russell Jr., was about 18 months old. I was living with his mom and we had no money, but I took my responsibilities seriously. I was trying to "be a man" and take care of my son and his mother, but I also knew I had to get an education. My family expected it. Though my mother had died while I was in my senior year of high school, she was big believer in education. In honor of her love of learning, I knew I had to get my degree.

I also had to get my degree so my father didn't kick my ass.

I was working all these jobs, trying to support my son. I needed every last cent to just to survive. I couldn't afford to get fired because my boss was so different from me. I couldn't afford to be out of a job the several weeks it might have taken me find another one. Instead, I needed to find a way to make that guy think I was "one of the good ones." I needed to make him like me so that my kid could eat.

Understand, it was a strategy. It wasn't that I *wanted* this guy to like me or that I cared what he thought of me deep down inside. No, I *needed* him to like me so I could take care of my own agenda and my own goals. As I will explain in Rule Number 14, goals can really hamper your ability to bullshit. Have as few of them as possible—and make sure the ones you *do* have are really, really good ones—like supporting your children and providing a good life for them.

Anyway, I needed this guy to like me, so I started listening to him. I listened to him when he talked about his interests. I noticed how excited he got when he talked about his favorite band, *Lynyrd Skynyrd* and how he knew all the words to "Freebird" when it came on the radio. I listened to him go on and on about NASCAR races and which drivers were likely to win which races.

Then, I went home and studied.

I listened to the rock station in my car and learned about *Lynyrd Skynyrd* and some of the other Southern rock bands of that time.

I read the articles about NASCAR on the Sports pages of the newspaper and the profiles of some of the drivers in *Sports Illustrated.*

Then, when I felt like I had something to say, I started adding a comment or two when he talked about those things.

"Yeah, it's really too bad about the plane crash," I said one day, when my boss was talking about *Lynyrd Skynyrd*. "Ronnie Van Zant was at the peak of his career." I shook my head sadly. "Talent like his doesn't come along every day."

Then I went back to what I was doing.

You should have seen the look on that dude's face!

He never expected me to know anything about *Lynyrd Skynyrd*. He expected me to hate Southern rock and only know about soul music, or God-forbid—*disco!* For me to say what I said about the plane crash that killed the band's lead singer in 1977 smashed the box he'd placed me in as a person.

He was both curious and confused by me. He was thinking, *"This guy may not be what I think he is. He might just be all right."*

That was exactly where I wanted him.

"Yeah," he stammered. "Losin' Van Zant really did 'em in."

For the rest of my shift, he kept staring at me like he didn't know what to make of me. By the next day, though, I noticed that I was suddenly included in his conversations. Just a day before, I'd been on the outside looking in.

Now, take note here, people. If you want to make people love you, you don't get up in their faces and start grinning and acting like a fool. You don't just agree with everything they say. You don't wander around going, "You like NASCAR? Wow! I do, too!"

That crap won't make *anyone* love you. Instead, everyone will see you for the big brown-noser that you are. Don't forget the things we talked about in Rule Number One. You never want your bullshit to be obvious or overdone. You want to be subtle. You want to be smooth.

To make people love you, you need two key techniques, and I demonstrated them both with this story. The first is to really pay attention to the person and genuinely try to figure them out. That means that you don't dismiss their interests out of hand. You don't grumble under your breath and turn up your nose, unless you just don't care whether you have a job or not. If you're smart about it—if you're playing the game—you'll keep your mouth shut and just listen. Then you'll go home after work and get your Google™ on.

If I had had Google™ back then, it would have made things so much easier, let me tell you. You have it, so you have no excuse. Listen and learn about what your boss is into, and when you have a good enough understanding to contribute something meaningful, employ the second key to this strategy, which is to offer your own information about the boss' favorite subjects, casually and calmly, like you and he (or she) have been discussing this stuff in a friendly way for years.

If you drop too much information, you're going to sound like an encyclopedia and the boss is going to know that you're playing a game. Once the boss figures out that you're gaming, you might as well just hand in your resignation. You're gonna be out of there soon enough anyway. It's all about being casual, easy and subtle.

How do you know if you've got it down?

Practice.

Sorry, that's all I've got for you. There's no magic wand here. You might have to overdo it and bear the consequences in order to learn to do it right. Since I've been full of bullshit my entire life, I already knew how to do this one.

Okay, I hear you. Here we go.

"But Russ," you're thinking. "Why do I gotta do all that? I'm not changing myself for *no one!*"

Okay, fine. I hope you're happy with where you're at

because guess what? You're staying there *forever*. If you decide you do want to get off fries at some point and get to the cash register, you might think about what I'm saying for just a minute. You might decide to try to see things just a little differently. You might decide to *do* things just a little differently. You might try to sprinkle your life with a little bullshit, and see what happens.

Sometimes that means that you will have to do some work. Sometimes you will have to focus on learning about *other* people. You may not know many people who come from a different cultural background than yours, but you'll have to lay down your preconceptions about them and learn. You'll have to do what I did with my auto parts manager and close your mouth and listen. You might have to do some research. You might have to reach beyond what you're used to in your own world to find out about another one.

That's how you make people love you. That's also how you play the game behind the game. Cash-checking is governed by rules that are bigger than your experience. Clinging to just what's normal for where you are right now won't get you a life beyond it.

OFF-COLOR JOKES

In our politically correct world, many bosses and supervisors wouldn't dare say the "N-word" out loud, but maybe you'll hear the one about the Mexican and the Black guy in the car together.

"Who's driving?" they'll ask, a big grin already spreading across their faces. "Who else? A cop!"

Hilarious.

Guess what I did when I heard that one (and others)?

I laughed.

I laughed like it was the funniest thing I ever heard.

Laughing at off-color jokes was something my father taught me. He despised it, but he knew it was how his White superiors tested him. The jokes were their way to find out how far they could go with him and whether they could trust him.

Remember, he was one of a very few Black officers in the Air Force and he was surrounded by White people. His advancement depended on them. He'd go out on the golf course with these White guys and laugh at their jokes, listening all the while to every word they said about what was happening on the job, or how they were increasing their net worth outside of it. He played the game—he was "one of the good ones"—and his efforts were rewarded by the kind of information he wouldn't have had access to if he'd gotten offended and started cussing them out. He got tips about real estate and invested in several properties that ended up increasing his bottom line. He got stock tips and started playing the market. He learned about the things men with power tell other men with power, and it enriched him and his family. Information like that has its cost, and for him, the cost was tolerating their bigotry.

Certainly, there is a place for calling out prejudice and insensitive comments, but I've got to be honest, sometimes people are really dumb about this. Instead of thinking about it coolly, rationally and playing the game, they just flip out. Think about it—yelling and screaming really doesn't change minds or correct attitudes or beliefs. But living well? Shattering stereotypes by achieving and succeeding? Those are the real game-changers.

When people say racially insensitive things to me, I usually don't react. Instead of calling them on it, I'm thinking, "Thank you for that. Now I know what you are and who you are." I start trying to figure out how to use that information to my advantage, which is something you really won't be able to do if you're too busy waving your finger in their faces and calling them "racist," or waiting for them in the parking lot with a ski mask on and a blunt object! Just kidding, of course. No one would actually do anything like *that!*

Sure, some people are classist, elitist, racist or even an ass-ist. (You do know I made that up, right?) But as I've said, telling them so doesn't change them, and it certainly doesn't get you anywhere. Doesn't it make more sense to try to figure out how manipulate their tendencies to help yourself?

DON'T BURN YOUR BRIDGES

Making the people in charge—and everyone else—love me has been a critical skill for me. I've found it important to make people love me in one way or another in all of my radio experiences. I worked "lovability" early in my career when I auditioned for TV commercials and had to charm casting directors. I even used this aspect of the game behind the game to get my first television show. Lovability opens doors, and if you don't know how to make people love you, you need to think seriously about the ways that you're putting people off. Are you argumentative? Are you difficult? Are you generally a jerk? Like the old folks used to say, "You'll kill more flies with honey than vinegar." My new rule, for cash-checking purposes is you'll collect more *cash* being nice to people than being an asshole. Being lovable also keeps you from burning bridges with people you might need in the future.

Before I was a radio jock in Dallas or Washington, DC, I was working with the legendary broadcaster, Steve Woods, at KDAY in Los Angeles and doing stand up in LA clubs at night. I had a reputation for being funny and for being able to pull off some pretty good impressions of some of the famous characters of the day. I would put on a Mohawk and imitate Mr. T. I could put on a single glove and sound like Michael Jackson. I could sound like Ronald Reagan. I was versatile and I had a good reputation.

While performing at an open mic night at The Comedy Store on Sunset Boulevard (the legendary comedy club where people like Jay Leno, Robin Williams, Richard Pryor and others started out), some producers saw me and I was offered the opportunity to work on *Rock 'N' America* with Canadian comic Rick Ducommun.

Rock 'N' America was a collection of the week's hottest rock videos with comedy bits dropped in between. It aired on Saturday nights after *Saturday Night Live*. We did all kinds of crazy stuff on that show, including all kinds of characters and bits, many of them things I'd played around with in comedy clubs for years. This was 1984.

Unfortunately, Rick ran into some problems and it was decided that he would have to be replaced. With a search for a new host underway, it seemed likely that I was out, too, since we had been a team. But then the show's producers selected Frazer Smith as the new host of *Rock 'N' America*. I knew Frazer. We'd worked together at KLOS. He insisted that I stay on *Rock 'N' America*.

Frazer loved me. Okay, that might be a bit much, but he at least *liked* me. If I had been an ass, I would have never been asked to stay on this national show. Lesson 1: Don't burn your bridges with people. You never know when you're going to need someone in the future. Lesson 2: Make *everyone* love you—or at least like you—even if they aren't your boss. You never know where the people you work with will end up.

To be fair, "Fraze," as we called him, was a cool White guy. It's important to learn where folk come from and Fraze was from Detroit. If you're White and from Detroit, you've had some dealings with some Black people, and Fraze and I started out pretty comfortable with each other. Still, I had worked on keeping a good relationship with him while we were both at KLOS. Working on *Rock 'N' America*, we picked up where we left off as co-workers and started writing and hosting together. I'm making it sound like we were equal partners, but in reality, I was the sidekick. I think I mentioned the importance of embellishment when one is looking for one's next opportunity? Wasn't that Rule Number One? Notice how I just dropped in my own little embellishment of my role in *Rock 'N' America?* Did you see how I promoted myself from "sidekick" to "co-host?" There isn't really a difference between the two, but for bullshit purposes, I went with co-host because it sounds bigger. If you don't understand why I might do that, you need to re-read Rule Number One.

The biggest thing about doing *Rock 'N' America* wasn't just the chance to do my comedy for a national audience. The biggest thing wasn't just that I was on TV. The biggest thing about doing *Rock 'N' America* was that it was an opportunity to introduce my comedy to a much wider—and whiter—audience. This is important because mine is an industry in which operating in "same-race" circles will only get you so far.

That's been true for me, and it's true for you, too.

There were once jobs or fields where you could achieve based entirely on your relationships with folks who look just like you, but these days that's no longer true. It's a multi-cultural world, and if you think of your career in only black or white terms, you're going to miss out.

President Obama knows what I'm talking about. I've had the honor to interview him a couple of times on the radio and, I'm telling you, he knows the rules of the game behind the game. Out of respect for him, in our interviews I've never focused on exposing this fact. That would be doing him an injustice. But understand, Mr. Obama is a brilliant man who knows how to straddle the fence of bullshit. He's a master at getting both Blacks and Whites to love him (and not because he's mixed). In fact, by the time some of the hardcore rednecks *figured out* he was Black, he was already elected! (That's pure bullshit on my part, by the way.)

I'm absolutely sure our President has a PhD in the Art of Bullshit, and don't sleep on the first lady, Michelle. She has mastered the game quite well, too.

I'll never forget when Tavis Smiley came on my show to complain because then-candidate Obama had declined an invitation to a convention he called the Black State of the Union. I'm sure he was also there to sell a book about his latest bullshit, too, but he was on my show about the Black State of the Union issue. This was during the election, so it must have been back in 2008.

"Hilary Clinton is going to be there. I don't understand why Barack Obama can't be there," he told my audience. He was all in huff about it. He was going on and on about how Obama was his "friend" and all that, but he didn't understand how Obama could be so disrespectful of Black people and blow off his event. (The President did offer the services of his wife, but to my understanding, Michelle Obama wasn't good enough.)

Tavis' complaints were pissing me off. I still don't understand why some Black people expect a hook up from another brother, like they are "owed" a response just because of common blackness. That's what it looked like at first, but there was something even more sinister going on. Let me break it down for you.

Here's Mr. Obama, a black man trying to show this nation that he can be President of *all* the people. Not just all the Black people, but *all* the people. I couldn't believe Tavis didn't understand that if Obama attended his convention, it would be just too easy for some (White) people to accuse him of *only* caring about Black folks. Not attending didn't mean he didn't care; it meant in the service of the greater good—getting elected as the first Black President in our nation's history—he had to decline. He was concentrating on getting the White people to love him so he could get his foot in the door and actually have the chance to *do* something for Black people!

Barack Obama was *playing* the game. What made me angry was that Tavis was *running* a game, in my opinion. He knew that if Obama attended the convention, it would have been suicidal to his Presidential bid. I felt at the time that Tavis had his own agenda. He set a trap, but Obama didn't bite. And Hilary Clinton? She had to love watching a "divide and conquer" strategy unfolding in front of her. If Tavis had succeeded, there may have been a nice little job for him in the Hilary Clinton administration. Too bad it didn't work! Oops!

"Playing the game" and "running a game" are two very different things, people. The level of deceit involved is different. When you're "playing the game," you may not always reveal all your motives, but your agenda is pretty clear. If you're on the job, it's about staying there or moving on to a better one. If you're looking for a job, it's about getting one. Obama was looking for a job—*the* job. His agenda was clear. He didn't reveal all his motives, but he didn't have to. He was playing the game to get to the desired result.

When you're "running a game," no one knows what your agenda is. You're concealing not just your motives, but exactly what your agenda is, too. Some felt that Tavis was in Hillary Clinton's pocket and that he wanted to see her get elected. So what? Just say so. "I'm for Clinton," he could have said. "And this is why you should be, too."

But no, his strategy was to run down the brother seeking the Presidency without revealing his own agenda. He wasn't trying to make us love him, and he certainly wasn't talking to the audience like they'd have sense enough to understand there were two fine candidates with good records for us to consider. No, instead he was almost saying, "Obama cares more about White people than he cares about you!" when the same criticism might have just as easily have been said about him.

The point is simply that you can think of my Rule Number Three, "Make People Love You," as some kind of Uncle Tom routine if you want. The reality is that it's such a big part of the game behind the game that the President himself used it to make history.

THE ART OF ADAPTING YOUR BULLSHIT TO MAKE EVEN MORE PEOPLE LOVE YOU

As I've said, I've been making people love me since I was a military kid facing a lot of preconceived notions about who and what I was. Even having reached the modicum (look it up!) of fame that I have achieved now, I'm still at it. Every day on the radio, I try to make my 67 listeners love me enough to tune in tomorrow. In some of my career experiences, this has been particularly hard.

Up until 1989, I had spent several years on the West Coast. There's a vibe there that is totally different than in other parts of the country. If I'd stayed there, I might never have realized that I had developed a style that only worked with a certain kind of audience. I didn't stay. When I left Los Angeles and accepted the job with KJMZ radio in Dallas, Texas, I learned for the first time that I had a problem.

The South was different. Texas was different. I had my assumptions about what it would be like to work in Texas. After all, I was born in San Antonio. The problem was, I didn't remember anything about the place. I'd never stayed in the state for any length of time, and most of what I thought I knew, I'd learned from TV.

The people in Dallas were much different than what I was accustomed to in LA. The mentality was extremely different. I have to admit, however, that I found Texans to be more honest than I was used to. Los Angeles, on the other hand, is a liar's town. If you live there, lying is something you have to get pretty damn good at, especially in the entertainment business.

"So what are you working on?" That's an LA question since, in LA, you're defined by what you're "working on." So, when the lady takes a breath after telling me about how she's starting a shoot with Spike Lee and Denzel next month, how her pilot got picked up by BET and her album will drop in June, I finish giving her my order and ask her to remove the appetizers from the table.

That's LA in a nutshell. It's not even bullshit, it's just lying. Lying is not bullshitting. Bullshit is saying and doing everything except lying. Lying is just lying. As you learned in Rule Number One, don't bother with bullshit that can be easily verified. It's much better to leave a little wiggle room in your pronouncements. What the waitress should have said was, "I'm up for a Spike movie and I did a pilot for BET that might be picked up. I'm also working on an album in my spare time." That description didn't contain even one out-and-out lie, but it leaves the listener with the bullshit impression that even though she's still waiting tables, she's got things rolling!

Okay, back to Dallas. Once I got there, I realized that LA bullshit really wouldn't work and that I really didn't know anything about Texas. And worse, Texas didn't know, or care, anything about me or my style of humor. As a comedian, when you find yourself having to *explain* your jokes to people, you know you have a serious, serious problem.

The solution?

Change.

Not the situation—though plenty of people try to solve their problems by trying to force their situation to change. When that doesn't work, they get all mad and throw up their hands. They start cussing and fussing. Either that, or they just quit.

"Y'all stupid! I'm outta here!"

Okay, that's not actually what they *usually* say. What they usually say is, "Fuck all y'all!" with as much attitude as possible. Either way, they quit and the situation stays the same.

There was a part of me that wanted to quit. There was a part of me that wanted to pack myself up and go back to LA where things had been going pretty good. At least I didn't have to explain my lies—I mean, my bullshit—there.

On the other hand, I'd chosen to take the opportunity in Dallas for a reason. I needed to do something different. I needed to challenge myself in new ways. Yes, I could have stayed in LA and probably would have made millions (okay, hundreds, but it's better than tens), but I'd never have met my wife. I'd never have had the radio career I've had. In those first few years, however, I couldn't figure out how to make the listeners in Dallas love me.

I had to figure out to how to be funny. Since I couldn't change them and *make* them "get me," I had to change myself.

This change wasn't as simple as a name change, like we discussed in Rule Number Two. It was much more drastic. I had to become them. I had to bullshit them into thinking I was a native. I had to make the show about them. I hired my soon-to-be best friend, Georgia Foy, a cute little intern from the University of Texas who was born and raised in Dallas. I changed her name to "Alfredas" (derived from her middle name Alfreda) to make her more relatable to an audience that might not have been as well-educated or as savvy as she was. We created her character as a South Dallas 'hood chick and developed a routine of playing off of the dynamic between us. We stuck with it, floating new bullshit out there every day and hoping some of it might make the audience laugh or stick in their minds. With Alfredas beside me, a lot of the bullshit started sticking. I got a whole new audience, and like my experience with *Rock 'N' America*, I found once again that if you make new people love you, you've made yourself more valuable. You're cash-checking on a whole new level.

My ratings began to soar.

Do you get me?

Here's the review for all of you that fell asleep after the first couple paragraphs of this chapter:

If you're going to succeed while Black, you have to

take the time to get to know people and make them love you. Make *everyone* love you. I mean you want to be pleasant and friendly to *everyone* from the CEO to the guys who clean the building at night. Why? Because you never, ever know who you might need later. That guy that works cleaning the office at night may be working on an invention on the side that might change the way we live, and when his company is hiring and you need to make a move, you want him to remember you as the guy or gal who knew his name and gave a shit about him when he was mopping the floor.

Making people love you includes being careful about the things you post on Facebook and Twitter. If you think that bullshit won't come full circle back to your office and bite you on your ass, you're fooling yourself. It's funny to me how many people think they can shit on you on the World Wide Web, then come and ask you for something in person! Don't say anything on the web that you wouldn't say to someone's face. Be pleasant and professional in what you say about supervisors, colleagues and your workplace online. Making people love you means, you *never burn your bridges.* Even if you think there's not a snowball's chance that your boss will see that Tweet, don't do it! Think of the Internet as an extension of your work persona, and you'll never be sitting in your boss' office trying to explain just why you managed to insult him or her in 140 characters or less.

Being pleasant to everyone at work is just good strategy. Good strategy leads to cash-checking, plain and simple. It sounds manipulative, but it's really not. It's really about *love*, people. I'm all about love, except for when money is involved.

RULE #4:

Black-sphemy: Look Out for the Man in the Mirror!

"The Man is keeping the brother down."

"I can't get anywhere because of the good ol' boys network."

"They got the game locked up."

I've heard these phrases more times than a few. While

I certainly wouldn't underestimate the role racism still plays in limiting opportunities for Black people, racism can't be your only concern. You've got to be worried about the other Black people in the office, too.

What's that you're saying—"Blasphemy, Russ Parr! Some things are sacred! How dare you write a book and criticize Black people!"

My response is simple. It's not blasphemy, it's black-sphemy (You can only get the joke here if you know what the words mean, but trust me, it's very clever!) I'll criticize Black people who can't stand to see other Blacks succeed all I want. That man in the mirror—that guy or gal who looks just like you—can be one dangerous, jealous mother^%$*, and it's my solemn obligation to call him out on it. That's why it's not "blasphemy," but "black-sphemy." My irreverence is for Blacks who hate on other Blacks.

You might have heard the phrase the old folks used: "acting like crabs in a barrel." If you've ever bought crabs, you know that they are alive until you cook them. When you buy them, they'll be climbing over each other and pushing each other down in their attempt to survive. More of them would actually be able to escape if they weren't so busy fighting each other, but they're crabs.

They don't reason. They don't think. Since they don't think, they don't escape.

Black folks do this to each other, too, and that's the reason why the phrase is so appropriate. We don't work together. We react emotionally to the appearance of someone getting ahead of us, and instead of realizing that every time one of us gets out of the "barrel" it means that there's one more person who is able to throw a ladder down to get more of us out, we instead try to grab them by the ankles and drag them back.

In the workplace, black-sphemy takes place on a daily basis. While you're trying to work your game and trying to get in a good position to get promoted, the brother sitting next to you is trying to figure out how to hold you back. While you're working your game to move on up the corporate ladder, the brother in the cube next door is grabbing you by the ankles, trying to drag you back, and usually not because he's after the same spot. Usually, he knows damn well that he doesn't have a shot at that job. He just doesn't want to see *you* have it. He doesn't want to see you climb out of the pot. It's not about fair competition between you for the same position. It's about petty jealousy. It's about, "If I can't have it, you can't either."

It's unfortunate, but it's true. It's happened to me.

At one of my radio jobs—I won't name the station or the market, because if I do they'll all know I'm talking about them—my co-worker was trying to get me fired before I even got started or established. I'm talking about doing really stupid stuff like having listeners write letters of complaint and slip them under the station manager's door. This person was telling the boss that I was doing stuff that I shouldn't have been doing on the air, and that the listeners weren't feeling me. That was actually more than likely true, but I know the boss had a radio, so the boss must have already known how I was doing. Then there was the "mole" who must have been following me around town, tipping management off to the things I was doing off the air, in the hope it would help convince them to show me the door. These things would have been just ridiculous if it hadn't been for the fact that if my bosses had fallen for this stuff, I would have lost my job. It might have at least made sense if these folks had any possibility of taking my place, or of getting the job that I had. They didn't. Rather, they were threatened by the very idea that I might succeed. Their beliefs about success were so narrow that they couldn't imagine a possibility in which I could be successful. They just wanted to try to drag me back into the barrel with the other crabs.

Crabs in a barrel, man. It's a nasty business. We've even see it play out on the national stage. Barack Obama is such a good example of this phenomenon that I have to talk about him once again.

Dr. Cornel West is one of America's most outspoken intellectuals. Never one to shy away from controversy, he has been a leading voice on politics, race, culture and religion for three decades. He is a published author and a frequent guest on the talk-show circuit. He also illustrates how the "crabs in a barrel" mentality operates at the highest levels of academic and intellectual life.

Dr. West had been critical of Barack Obama on a number of occasions. I don't have a problem with anyone being critical of our President, but as I pointed out earlier, it's important to take note of the agenda of the critic. Dr. West has stated in the past that the President has to walk a political tightrope that is higher and narrower than any other President has ever had to walk, but recognizing the difficulties of his balancing act hasn't stopped Dr. West from trying to trip Obama up on his high wire act.

I was very surprised to see him on TV taking shots at the President since Dr. West has built his entire career on advocating for the advancement of the Black man. What had Barack Obama done to Cornell West for him to be receiving calculated public tongue lashings from this well-respected Black intellectual?

Well, I did a little research . . . and ah ha! There was indeed a reason!

The President had hurt Dr. West's feelings.

Apparently, Dr. West was invited to the White House. When he arrived, the President made a beeline to Dr. West and proceeded not to congratulate him or gush over him, but instead to express his disappointment about some of the disparaging comments he'd made in the media about the President and his agenda. According to the sources I found, Dr. West was quoted as saying, "Frank Rich, Paul Krugman, Maureen Dowd, and a whole host of brilliant, courageous critics say all kinds of things and he treats them with respect. They get invited to the White House. I say the same things, and he talks to me like I'm a Cub Scout."

Dr. West had been critical of the President, and the President wasn't happy about it, so he had a few words for him. If he was singled out for comments by the President, I see Dr. West's point. These other (White) people were critical of the President, too, and yet, when they got invited to the White House, the President didn't say a word to them about their comments. Dr. West goes to the White House and gets a talking to.

It doesn't seem fair.

When I look at the whole picture, Dr. West, I see it a little differently. The difference between you and those other critics is that they have a lighter tan. I believe the President *expects* their criticism. He probably *didn't* expect yours, especially given that your platform has always been one of Black advancement. Here's a Black man who has reached the pinnacle of national office—he's the leader of the Free World—and he can't get any love from you? Is there any higher "Black advancement" than what this brother has accomplished? What on earth *more* do you want from him?

Dr West had a bruised ego and, like Tavis Smiley—and this is just my humble opinion—he was on some type of "get back." Both Dr. West's ego and the President's ego are evident here, and certainly both of them are accomplished Black men, but whenever I see Dr. West on

TV taking shots at the President, I have a better understanding of what lies just beneath his comments. The difference between Dr. West and the President is that the President didn't use the media to put Dr. West on blast. He confronted him privately. For a while, it seemed Dr. West wasn't taking the same approach, though lately, I have noticed that Dr. West is defending the President more often.

This exchange between two successful Black men is an example of black-sphemy. Personally, I liked Dr. West best when he was saying things like, "The Black evolution of the imperial solitude has evidentualized the metamorphosis of a metaphor incongruently, decimating the methodical upliftment of the disenfranchisement of the Black man."

Deep, huh?

No, Dr. West never said anything like that. I made that up, but he does say some shit like that. And will you get an edge up, damn it? Go read some books or something, so you aren't embarrassing yourself!

One more on the President, and then I'm going to talk about myself, I promise.

Remember when Jesse Jackson was on Fox News

before the election of 2008? Mr. Jackson didn't know his microphone was on and he was whispering to another guest that Barack Obama was talking down to Black people. He said something like, "Speaking to them on this faith based . . . I want to cut his nuts off." The President is still getting those kinds of comments. These are the same people who are saying now, "Obama's an elitist! Obama's a classist. He don't care about us!"

What do you want?

The guy got a good education and used it wisely. Now he's "elitist" and "thinks he's White" because he got a little something to show for using his brains, for doing the hard work and for making good decisions?

Seriously?

When Reverend Jackson accused the President of "talking down to Black people," he was raising the cry that Obama was an "elitist." When you think about it, Reverend Jackson was actually saying something about himself. Now the good Reverend couldn't possibly have been jealous of the then Senator from his hometown, could he? No, of course not! Not even because, years before, Reverend Jackson had attempted his own (unsuccessful) bids for president? Not even because Obama was generating an excitement that transcended racial boundaries? Not even because Obama had a chance at the office that Jackson had failed to achieve?

Jealous?

No way! Not Jesse Jackson! He's a preacher! Preachers don't feel jealous! (They also don't "cut people's nuts off," or at least they're not supposed to.)

Needless to say, Jackson's comments didn't help Obama very much, and unfortunately, they didn't help Reverend Jackson very much either. Just like crabs in a barrel, these sorts of "I'm not going to help you succeed" words and actions don't help anyone. Black folks keep doing them to each other, throughout all economic levels, all industries, all kinds of workplaces, and all kinds of opportunities. All we achieve is that we keep dragging each other down.

THINKING "WHITE"

I'm not the President, but I'm a Black man who's made the most out of the talents I have. Sometimes, I get the same kinds of criticisms.

"How come Russ got that? He kissing the man's ass, that's why. He thinks he's White, that's why."

Uh, no. I don't think I'm White. I don't think that at all. I know exactly what I am and where I came from. In Rule Number Eight, you'll hear some of my stories about encounters with cops. White people don't have stories like that. I've already told you about how many jobs I've had where my White bosses' first instincts were to try to get me fired because I was Black. They embraced all the negative stereotypes about Black people—that we're lazy and shiftless and criminals and stupid. I've worked all my life to prove those stereotypes to be completely wrong. As soon as you start to succeed—the harder you work to show that you're not what White people think Black people are—you get Black people muttering that "you think you're White." If you think you're White then, that means you either have to stop doing whatever it was that got you where you are in life, or you owe a piece of what you've earned to every Black person who passes by with their hand out.

This whole idea of "thinking White" is really a sad commentary on what some people believe about what it means to "think Black" or to be Black, for that matter. If being successful means you think you're White, then that seems to suggest that that to be Black is to be unsuccessful. I hope that it isn't true, but I've heard that I "think I'm White" enough times to wonder about it. Do some of us really believe that getting an education, making the most of our talents and then getting some money in our pockets is selling out blackness?

What kind of blackness do you people believe in? Don't you know that we are a tradition of hardworking people who value education and success? Don't you know you are the descendants of achievers and builders, of scholars and strivers? If you don't know, you need to know. Get on Google™. Or even better, go to school.

Succeeding while Black is tough because you're damned if you do and damned if you don't. You get squeezed by some White people because you're Black, and you get squeezed by some Black people because you're successful.

I've only been sued once, and it was by Black people who had this idea that if you see a Black person who has something, he owes you some of it.

While I was working in Dallas, I created *Flava TV,* which was similar to *Rock 'N' America* in that it was a collection of videos and comedy bits, but aimed at an African American audience. The show had been on for a couple of years and was doing pretty well.

This Black couple wanted to buy some advertising time on the show, which they did, but then they claimed they were promised a segment on my show to do whatever they wanted.

Say what? Whatever you want? I would have *never* approved that, but they insisted that that was what they were told, and when I refused to give them a segment, they took me to court, alleging that I reneged on a promise. By now you know I'm the "I want everyone to love me" guy. When I realized they sincerely felt that they were entitled to something, I tried to compromise. I gave them more advertising for free, hoping that this would ease their hurt feelings. They took the free ads, but I still got served.

I really didn't see that coming. I was surprised by it. I really didn't expect the situation to end up in court. I never expected to be sued by anyone, but certainly not by Black people who were fans of the show—or at least they said they were. Of course there really wasn't any legal basis for their lawsuit. There wasn't a contract for anything more than buying advertising, and in court, it didn't matter what they thought they were promised. There just wasn't any legal basis for what they wanted and they lost.

The whole situation was just crazy and I was really angry. It bothered me that I was trying to do something positive, and these people just took advantage of my good intentions. My anger ate at me for days and days. Finally, I was out jogging, still mulling over this whole mess with these people over in my mind, and finally I just said to myself, "I forgive them."

It was like a weight was lifted off my shoulders. I really understood, for the first time, the power of forgiveness. It really was an amazingly freeing moment for me, and since then, I've been able to call upon it many times. Believe me, I've needed to.

"Russ Parr! You rich! Buy me a car."

Let's say I buy them a car (okay, so that's not going to happen, but I'm telling a story here, so go with it.) I buy the car, but are they happy?

"Russ, you bought me car, but you didn't give me no gas to put in it, so what good is it?"

Some people are never satisfied. Some White people aren't satisfied either, but we're talking about some of the attitudes that plague the Black community, and to me it's another form of black-sphemy that some of us can't stand to see others get any kind of financial advantage.

That couple who sued me and tried to get every penny that *Flava TV* had ever earned thought I was rich because I was on the radio and because I had a TV show. They didn't know that I wasn't rich, that I'd invested everything I had in *Flava TV,* and that the show was in debt to the tune of $100,000. They just saw someone Black trying to do something, and thought they could cash in.

Other times, with Black folks, the game is competitive materialism. You know what I'm talking about. It's the "Oh, you got a Cadillac so I'm getting a Mercedes" stuff. It's the "You got a three-bedroom house, I'm gonna get me a six bedroom crib with gold-plated toilet seats." It's bullshit, and not the good kind. Just like the folks who think they are owed some of other Black people's success, competitive materialism is just another version of the crabs in a barrel mentality. You got ahead of me, I'm gonna get ahead of you. You crawled over me, I'm crawling over you. We're getting all into one-upping each other with *things,* when we should be thinking about responsible saving and investing.

Did you know that African Americans spend $520 *billion* a year? $520 billion! (On Mercedes Benz's. Just kidding. We also buy Gucci and Cristal!) Can you imagine what we could do if we just spend a fraction of those billions on community uplift? Just a fraction of those billions on wealth building for the next generation? Just a fraction of those billions on creating our own businesses?

Instead, we just spend and we spend a lot. We spend most of it on trying to make ourselves look richer than the crab right behind us in the barrel.

I really don't like this, and I try not to play into it. As I've said, my family was middle class and had more than many of the Black families that I knew growing up. As a kid, I tried to downplay any economic differences between me and other kids. Certainly, my father wasn't the kind of man who ran around trying to impress people with the things he had. We didn't have luxury items. He wasn't into that. To this day, I'm not a label-conscious person. I don't wear a lot of jewelry. You won't catch me with some diamond-ed watch or sporting gold chains, teeth or rings. I'm not into clothes, either. I'll wear the same old jeans for five days. Yeah. I'll wear a pair of jeans until they hurt, and they aren't designer jeans either. Now, I admit, I do like cars, but that's as far as my materialism goes.

Today, we've got kids shooting and killing each other over jewelry and jeans and all kinds of silly possessions. Life is infinitely more important than any item that you might wear on your body or own. It's sad that we've reached such a state that the crabs will kill over some material item.

Now, I'm not painting all Black people as guilty of committing black-sphemys. I'm not calling all Black folks "crabs in a barrel." Not all Black people are like that. In case you haven't figured it out by reading this book, I'm suspicious of everyone—regardless of color. That's a part of how I play the game!

Too many times, I've had Black people walk up to me and say, "You're doing great things!" and as soon as I walk away, they're running me down. "He had a hook up." "He knew somebody, that's how he got where he is today." "He's got something on the boss. Yeah, he got pictures of the dude in a dress or something."

Why do I have to have a "hook up?" Why can't it just be that I'm talented and I work hard and that's why I'm successful? Why is that? It's frustrating.

Part of perfecting the art of bullshit is accepting that race isn't a predictor or a protection. Anyone can be an ally and anyone can be a backstabber. Race is only one of the many cards in the deck that can be played against you, and that race card can be played by people who look different from you or by people who look just like you.

RULE #5:

Work Hard—Or Give the Appearance That You Are Working Hard!

(No One Will Notice if You Wear Baggy Pants)

"Man, you wouldn't believe what they wanted me to do!"

"I ain't going to work at no McDonald's. Forget *that!*"

"That's not in my job description."

Some folks *love* to tell you what they aren't going to do. That's one of the reasons why some of us aren't doing anything at all.

When you need work, no job is too small. When you need to a keep a job, no job is too small. When you want to move up from the job you're in, no job is too small. The willingness to do whatever it takes is what wins you the most money in the end. The attitude that you're "too good" for some kinds of work will never earn you the big bucks. Instead, it will keep you from cash-checking at all.

Once again, you're probably saying,"Yeah, Russ Parr. If I had *your* job, I'd be willing to take on extra, too. You got a great job. Nobody's asking you to swish the toilet bowl. You making big money, so that's fine for you."

Yeah, it's fine for me. I work a lot. I get up at 4 am to do *The Russ Parr Morning Show* five days a week. When I'm not doing that, I write screenplays and direct movies. When I'm not doing those things, I'm speaking at schools or shuffling my kids from one event to another with the help of my wife, Darnell. We are human taxi services, believe it.

I don't sleep on opportunities, and I mean that literally. Most nights, I only sleep a few hours. I love my work, and my mind is always turning on new ideas. I recently came up with an idea about how I could make some money by writing a book about bullshit. Unfortunately, I couldn't get the idea off the ground. Too bad. It probably would have been a bestseller!

I've always been a hard worker, pursuing multiple ideas at the same time. I had that work ethic from the beginning, long before there was a *Russ Parr Morning Show*, before I was working with TV-ONE, before I created *Flava TV* back in the 1990s, and before I was doing stand up and creating many of the characters I'm known for today.

It's something my parents instilled in me, years and years ago. They were both hardworking people. My mother went back to school to become a teacher in her thirties. My father had his salary from the Air Force, but he was always investing and looking for additional opportunities. When I was a young adult, my father offered me some help and support, but only when I truly needed it. He knew that life wasn't a free ride and that if I wanted something, I needed to be willing to work hard to get it.

My parents' example taught me from an early age that life wasn't going to hand me anything. Instead, I'd have to work to obtain my opportunities or work to create them for myself. That's why the third strategy in perfecting the art of bullshit and playing the game behind the game is that hard work leads to good work, which leads to better work. Don't be deceived—all of it is work and all of it has its difficulties. At the end of the day, there really isn't "better work" or "worse work." Work is work is work.

BABY ON BOARD

I have always worked hard. I wasn't a great student in high school, but I played basketball and I knew I had to keep certain grades if I was going to be allowed to play. I thought I was working hard, balancing work and sports. I didn't have a clue.

I didn't have that much sexual experience back in my high school days, and I was really naïve about it, so I guess that's how I ended up becoming a father while I was in high school. I remember how scared I was. My mother had died earlier that year, so I was a lost soul. I was angry at God for a very long time. I will say this much about fatherhood—when it comes to stepping up and being responsible for your children, do *not* apply the art of bullshit. Children need what's real from you, not something manipulative or manufactured. You don't want your kids to "like" you. You want them to respect you, and that only happens when you spend real time with them, really listening and really caring about what's going on in their lives.

Off the soap-box, and back to cash-checking.

As a teenaged father trying to do what was right, I had dozens of difficult, demanding and back-breaking jobs. I can't even remember how many jobs I've had, there've been so many. I already told you about the auto parts store, but one of the other ones that I remember was taking inventory for a local grocery store chain. I had to get up at 3 am and go out to the store, where I was fitted with this little tabulator that I wore on my hip. Then, I'd stand in the store going up and down the aisles, clicking and counting boxes of cereal or sanitary napkins or cartons of ice cream. One, click. Two, click. Three . . . I didn't click on the things that I "borrowed" from the store, since I had every intention of paying for them at a later date. In fact, there's a check in the mail right now—bank on it.

My father gave me the job of collecting rent and keeping the books at some properties he owned, in exchange for living space while I attended Merced Junior College. If I were to put a title on it, I guess I would say I was an apartment manager. The tenants figured me out real fast. My dad will never admit this because he likes to think of himself as a hard ass, but he has a soft side, too. It was his softer side that sent me out there to manage his property. He knew I had lessons to learn about dealing with people. He wanted me to learn how to be a hard ass when it came to collecting the rent.

He didn't get caught up in people's stories about why they couldn't pay. He expected the rent. I, on the other hand, would fall for just about any excuse. All they had to do was come to me crying, and I'd tell them it would be okay. Then I'd have to take money from one of my *other* part-time jobs to try and cover what was missing so my father wouldn't be all over me about not doing my job.

"You're just like your mother," he would say, but there would be just the hint of a smile on his face. I think he liked seeing that compassion in me. It reminded him of Mom.

Betty Ann Parr was the kindest, most generous person to ever grace this earth. If there was a stray cat with rabies spitting poison on the street, we were allowed to bring it home and try to nurse it back to health. I can't remember how many times my mom would use her salary from her teaching job to bail a neighborhood kid out of jail! She just cared about everyone. When I was about 13, I had a paper route and my mom would get up 3 o'clock in the morning and help me wrap my newspapers. Then, she'd follow me in the car while I threw papers from my bicycle. Even back then, my mom instilled a work ethic in me. She could have easily driven me and let me throw papers out of the window of the car on those freezing mornings, but then she would have been doing *my* job. She let me do it on my own, but followed along behind me in the car, just in case.

The newspaper job is just another example of how my parents shaped my work ethic. Later, I once had a job telemarketing, trying to sell people something, I can't even remember what. I had a job at Castle Air Force Base in Atwater, California working in the Officer's Club washing dishes in the club restaurant. I'd go in near the close of dinner service and there would be dishes and pots piled nearly to the ceiling. Just hundreds of plates, cups, bowls, pots and pans. It wasn't my only job, so I'd have already worked another job before going there, and attended school, too. I'd be there for hours and hours, just exhausted, trying to melt that pile of dirty dishes down to none. Occasionally, I would throw dishes away. I know that wasn't right, but it accomplished two important things—it made my bosses think I was a fast worker and it made my night shorter. Now that is some *serious* bullshit at work right there.

Those jobs were hard and horrible, but the hardest job I ever had wasn't one of the ones where physical labor was involved. The hardest job I ever had was doing stand-up comedy.

People think living the "artist life" is easy and fun, but, as I've said before, comedy is brutal. The only thing I imagine that might be worse is boxing, which tears up your body like comedy shreds your soul. Comedy is about making people laugh, but there's nothing funny about the lives most comedians live. It truly is a soul-crushing business. One night, you're killing. Everyone's laughing and they love you. The next night, with a different audience and the exact same material, they're booing you and throwing stuff at the stage. You don't even know what happened. It just rips your heart out.

Even worse, there's no money in it. You do it for love,

not cash-checking. Most comedians never make more than a few bucks. Most comedians never get TV sitcoms or movie deals. Most never become headliners on the national circuit. Instead, they become drug addicts and alcoholics, and some of them just blow their brains out. I'm not bashing them; I understand it completely. I can remember having to take a drink just to go out there, and feeling it burning in my stomach while I performed. I remember sweating under the lights, knowing that tomorrow I'd have to go back to my day job. No, comedy isn't about cash-checking. It's not the money that makes me or the other guys and gals get up there and do it.

We do it for the laughs.

When someone laughs—when someone thinks you're funny—it's almost worth it. Almost. Comedy is unbelievably hard work—the hardest work I've ever done. Still, I approached even comedy with a certain work ethic.

Fortunately, in most careers, a good work ethic and the determination to stay with the work even when it gets difficult, will ultimately help you play—and even win—the game behind the game. Being willing to put in that hard work leads to cash-checking, better opportunities and succeeding while Black. The harder you're willing to work, the better you're likely to do.

A GOOD WORK ETHIC OPENS DOORS

I've never had the attitude that any job was beneath me. As my experience has grown, I've sought out opportunities that use my talents, my background and my interests more fully. When I was young and had no experience and only the rawest kind of talent, I worked wherever they would hire me, and was glad to be employed.

When I first entered the job market, I already had the adult responsibilities of a family. My son's mother was in nursing school, and her schedule wasn't flexible. Childcare responsibilities fell to me, as well as the financial burden of supporting us. We only had one car, a little Pinto that she drove to school. I ended up taking the bus around town to work and to school, sometimes with my then one year old son (Russell Jr.) in one those baby harness things strapped on my back. It was rough, but it was what I had to do.

Unfortunately, the stress of trying to carry all those responsibilities was just wearing me down. I kept at it for about a year, and then, after a really tough week, I knew I'd had enough. I decided to drop out of school and just focus on work. They were dead end jobs, but at that point I was starving. I was living almost entirely off of fatty hamburger meat and canned green beans because they were cheap. I was stealing from cash registers to keep my son in formula. I was exhausted all the time and I just didn't think I could keep it up long enough to finish my degree.

I got the paperwork to drop out, and I went to Dr. Woods, who, as head of the department and my advisor in Radio, Television and Film, had to sign off on my decision.

"I'm dropping out. I can't handle all this anymore. I've got to take care of my kid," I told him.

He stared at me for a long time.

"No. You're not dropping out. I am not going to let you drop out."

He was serious. He refused to sign the paperwork. Instead, he used his influence on campus to help me. He got me additional work-study jobs so that I could earn some money on campus and not have to take the bus all over town to get to a bunch of different jobs. He also let me bring little Russ to class with me. Little Russ was such a good baby. He hardly ever cried and loved to let everyone play with him. Dr. Woods' tolerance for a small child in his classroom might have worn out quickly if the kid was crying all the time, but Little Russ was good and so was I.

As I said, I had a bunch of dead end jobs and I struggling to make it, but I believe that was why Dr. Woods was willing to help me. If I'd just said, "to hell with it" and gone down to the corner to smoke weed with my boys instead of taking every job that I could, trying to provide for myself and my family, I never would have gotten his help. If I'd said to myself: I've got this kid now, so I'm just gonna give up on going to school, I would have never even *met* him. If I'd just abandoned the mother of my child and focused on *me,* I don't think he would have respected me as much as he did, seeing me with my child in a harness on my back as I struggled to do everything I could to work and stay in school.

The fact that I was willing to work at several low-paying, menial jobs in order to handle my responsibilities revealed something important about my character. It spoke to my self-definition and told the story of the kind of man I wanted to become. Dr. Woods saw that in me. It made him willing to help me out. Indeed, he became my mentor for the remainder of my school career. Wherever he is, I owe him a tremendous debt of gratitude. Since I can never repay him, I'll try to pay it forward by sharing what I've learned with you.

You never know where a small, low-paying job might lead you. I don't care if you work at a fast food joint mopping the floors—and I've mopped floors, so I know what that's like—if you do it carefully and well, someone will notice. Next thing you know, you'll be promoted to dropping the French fries and after that, you might be managing the whole restaurant, and from there, buying a franchise of your own!

Work is work is work. All of it can be hard, and all of it has its rewards, if done well. Not only does being willing to work hard reveal your character, it also develops character, too. You learn a lot when you have to persevere in the face of hardship or obstacles. You learn whether you're a quitter or a fighter.

More than once in those years when I was struggling with work and school and fatherhood, I wanted to quit. I wanted to quit because it was so difficult. I wanted to quit because I just didn't see how I could physically stand to do what I was doing anymore. I nearly missed out on a big opportunity because I just didn't think I could keep all the balls in the air. (There is a "balls" joke I could insert here but I'm not going to do it. Y'all probably already think I'm "nuts." Well, I managed to slip a joke in anyway. Did you miss it? Really, you're going to have to expand your horizons if you hope to appreciate such cutting humor!)

It was in my second to last semester at Cal State Northridge that I bullshitted my way into that job in production services at KABC-TV. Remember that one? The story about how I told the HR Director that I needed his help with a paper, but I really just wanted to give him my resume? The one I talked about in Rule Number One—"A Little Bit of Bullshit Goes a Long Way?"

Are you paying attention? Look, if you're not going to *read* this damn book, what's the sense in me writing it? For those who are still awake, I will continue.

Well, I got a job from that stunt, but I almost didn't take it.

It was the first opportunity that I'd gotten in the field where I hoped to make my career, and I really wanted to accept it. The problem was, it was a real, nine-to-five job and I just didn't see how I could work there, continue my home responsibilities and still take 21 credits at school. It just seemed impossible. I was just one semester shy of graduation and I didn't want my school work to suffer. I wanted to graduate.

I was going to turn the job down, but I decided to talk to Dr. Woods first.

"Take the job," he said.

I explained to him all my concerns.

"You'll be all right. Take the job. It's a great opportunity, and if you don't take it, you'll regret it. You might not get another chance to get your foot in the door. It'll be hard, but you're used to that, right?"

I took it. He was right—it was hard. On top of my difficult personal balancing act, I had the problems with my supervisors that I told you about that almost got me fired. Taking the job with ABC-TV led to the opportunity to work for KABC radio, however, and radio was something I knew I wanted to do. So, Dr. Woods was right. It all worked out, and one of the reasons why was because, once again, he went to bat for me. In the middle of the semester, Dr. Woods petitioned the dean to have all my day classes moved to night classes. That schedule change allowed me to work by day, and do that last semester of class by night. I often think about how different things would have been for me if I had dropped Dr. Wood's class because he was too hard.

When the opportunity came to interview with KABC-Radio, I wasn't sure I would get the job. I just knew that I wanted it. It was in the field that I already knew was what I really wanted to be in, but I was in a mess at KABC-TV. The guy at HR who set up the interview discouraged me. He didn't think I had a chance, but I knew I wanted to do that job, so I went anyway.

I worked my bullshit. I was charming and confident. I said I knew how to do things I wasn't sure I knew how to do, but I was sure I would learn how to do them. I told charming (and true) stories about how, in junior college, I worked for the college station. I told the charming and true story about how I worked at KLBS radio in a small town called Los Banos where I had my own show for a little while. I impressed them with my charming (and true) stories. I got the job.

However uncertain they might have been about hiring me—I was, after all, just out of college and really didn't have much experience—I made sure they didn't regret it. How? I worked my ass off. I was working 50–52 hours in only three and half days of the week. I was bouncing between programs at KABC talk radio and at KLOS, the affiliated rock station. I was constantly getting sick. My schedule and my home responsibilities meant that I was constantly on the go, and even though I had been used to working lots of hours, my responsibilities at my earlier jobs hadn't had as much stress associated with them. I needed more rest, but I didn't take it. I knew I had things to prove, so I started doing male exotic dancing on the side, in addition to working the ungodly hours at the . . . just kidding.

I worked harder. They learned that I was good. They learned that I could do creative things with the board that would enhance the shows. They learned that I was good with sounds and voices. They learned that I wrote comedy bits, so soon I was being asked to produce commercials for the account managers.

I ran the board for Dr. Laura Schlessinger when she used to fill in for Dr. Toni Grant, one of the first psychologists to have an advice show on radio. There was a little battle brewing between Dr. Toni and Dr. Laura because Dr. Laura was already trying to get her own show. Everybody knows what happened when she finally did—her infamous "nigger, nigger, nigger, nigger" diatribe forced her to retire from her nationally-syndicated advice show in 2010. At the time, I didn't know she harbored racist thoughts—she never showed me her neck—but I guess I probably should have figured it out. KABC was a conservative radio station and attracted listeners who often embraced negative stereotypes about Black people.

KABC was also the flagship radio station for the Los Angeles Dodgers. I used to go the stadium and run the board for the late, great sportscaster Bud Furillo. We used to leave during the seventh inning stretch and we'd have to get back in time to the post-game show. We'd go to his house, which wasn't too far from the stadium, and smoke weed. Yes, weed. He was a lot older than me—he must have been in his late fifties or sixties and I was in my twenties—but we'd be there at his house, smoking weed. Then we'd go back and do the post-game show, laughing and laughing and laughing. Bud Furillo was a good guy. He saw that I was hard worker, and he respected that. He introduced me to a lot of people, including Tommy Hawkins who was Vice President of Communications and External Affairs with the Dodgers, and was a really well-known Los Angeles sportscaster—as well as a former Los Angeles Laker. He also worked at KABC doing sports. I used to make Tommy laugh.

I also worked on *Ken Bob and Company*, KABC Radio's top-ranked talk program. On their daily talk show, Ken Minyard and Bob Arthur talked to people, all kinds of people, from all walks of life. Their show was on the air for almost two decades, and they were truly the best at their craft. Listening to them talk and debate with their guests was learning from the top guys in radio, and everything I know about interviewing people, I learned from listening to them.

For years I always heard "Black people don't want to talk about issues," and I never believed it. I've always had to press to discuss topics on my shows because that idea is still out there. Even now, though my shows are music intensive, I'm not afraid to talk and bring in guests with points of views and challenge them on it. It's something that I picked up during that early experience at KABC, working on *Ken Bob and Company.*

I worked with Lee Marshall, a newscaster at KABC Radio with a really deep "radio-sounding" voice. His is the voice on that "Stop the Violence" song a lot of rappers got together to produce in the mid-1990s. He's the one who introduced me to stand-up comedy by using his connections to get me the chance to open for Joan Rivers at a club in Santa Monica. Of course, this was after I spent weeks writing an act and performing it around the hallways of ABC-Radio until I was sure it was good.

The point is that doing good work makes a positive impact in the workplace. It gives people the confidence in you to recommend you for bigger and better opportunities. We'll get to recommending people later, in Rule Number Seven, but for now, the point is that hard work builds the kind of reputation you need if you want to succeed while Black.

WORKING WHILE PLAYING

"Hey, man, let's go to lunch!"

"Let's hit happy hour!"

"We want to take you to dinner tonight."

These words are among my least favorite words at the office. Along with "We just want to talk to you about something" and "We need to have a short meeting."

I dislike these phrases because they are usually accompanied by an agenda—someone *else's* agenda. I really don't like other people's agendas. They usually contain nasty surprises. Work is work is work, and you always expect to be playing the game when you're working. Lunch, happy hours and dinner dates, even with friendly co-workers, present problems. Lunch is never just lunch. Happy Hour is filled with perils. Dinner dates aren't just social. Meals and drinks are where employees practice their games on each other. If you think these gatherings are just about eating some food or having some drinks, well, you're either extremely naïve or you haven't been paying attention.

Socializing with co-workers and superiors is like navigating Afghanistan's mine fields. They are encounters filled with unseen bombs. One wrong step and BOOM! They are opportunities designed to tempt you to forget yourself and reveal your game. If you have to hang out, especially with the boss, but even with other co-workers, remember one key rule:

You are still at work.

When I was hanging out in bars with my boss from the auto parts store listening to *Freebird*, man, I was at work.

When I was smoking weed with Bud Furillo, I was still at work.

Years later, when I was drinking with my radio co-host, Steve Woods, I was still at work.

When I'm invited to fancy restaurants or golf courses with the people who are my superiors even now, I treat them not as social opportunities—even if that's what they are *supposed* to be—but as an extension of my job persona.

I've heard plenty of Dumb Negro Syndrome ("DNS" for those of you who don't know) stories of people who forgot that hanging out with people from work is still work. They get drunk and shoot their mouths off and say something that isn't part of the bullshit they're supposed to say. Instead, they say some bullshit they really mean.

"You're such a stupid motherfucker, if I didn't cover your ass they'd have fired you a long time ago!" Insert loud drunken laughter here. "I oughtta have your damn job."

Then they wonder why the morning after, they've got a hangover and a pink slip.

Or they think they can "trust" someone enough to tell them about that really good idea they have about how to improve things in the workplace and then are surprised when the next day, in some meeting, that person offers the very suggestion that they'd been developing for months.

There is no "hanging out" with people from work. It's still work. Believe that and treat it accordingly.

This is not to say that you become the asshole of the office. You don't want to be the weird guy or girl who never speaks to anyone and refuses all invitations. You don't want to be completely anti-social. You always want to be pleasant. You want to speak to everyone. You want to work that second rule, the one where you "make everyone love you." If they love you, they won't start hating on you because you don't go to lunch every day and happy hour every night. They might even be happy for you when you get promoted over them because you work so hard. Okay, maybe they won't be happy, but there won't be anything they can do about it.

Every now and then, you should definitely join your co-workers or your boss for a social event. Just don't have fun. *Be* fun, but don't *have* fun. Save that for your real friends and your family. Remember that work is work is work. Also, avoid rodeos, bungee jumping, sky-diving and hunting for deer. Accidents happen.

Lunching and socializing can be ways to work your game, but I prefer the good old fashioned alternative of *working hard.* I believe in working, in going the extra mile and in taking on more than is expected of you. I might have socialized a bit, and I still do, but no amount of socializing would have ever been enough to take me to the next level—and it won't do it for you, either. What takes you to next level is being good at what you do and proving yourself to be hard-working, versatile and capable.

CREAM RISES

Does anyone even know where that expression "cream rises" came from? Something about the milk on the top of a bottle? Is that good? No? Okay, let's try this one for my militant brethren. It's a metaphor for the White man who always rising above the disenfranchised Black person who will never catch a break because of the hue of his skin. Does that sound better? No? Well, it doesn't matter since I'm not talking about that either.

I'm talking about the fact that bosses always notice the person who's always reliable, always supportive, always willing to go the extra mile, and always prepared. Make that person *you* by being willing to work hard, by extending yourself, by being that go-to guy or girl in whatever work environment you find yourself.

Being a hard worker makes you creative. It means that you never really leave work behind. Your mind is always turning and churning with ideas. You're committed enough to spend even your free time researching, thinking and coming up with new ways to do things.

In my own experiences, my love of radio and comedy kept me engaged with the medium. I listened to Wolfman Jack and Rick Dees and what they were doing with pop and rock, and I tried to bring that, along with my own ideas, to Black radio. I was probably one of the first Black DJ's to really bring sound effects and laugh tracks and voices and noises into my radio show. My shows sounded like there were fifteen people in the studio when really it was just me and all my noises, characters, sounds effects and bits. A lot of what I was doing wasn't entirely spontaneous. I had to take the extra time to find those sounds and put them together. I had to take the extra time to record those voices and bits, and it wasn't company time. It was *mine*.

The result is that, over the years, I've built something that's unique and recognizable as my own. *Now* it's a brand, but *then*, it was just me fooling around in my off-hours with ideas. To this day, I run my own board. I know how to create the timing that makes a Russ Parr show. I'm happy to do that work, and it's not a job that I consider beneath me. I consider it important enough not to ever delegate it to anyone else.

If you're not getting anywhere in your professional life, you've got to ask yourself some questions like: Am I really working at it? Am I working at it hard enough? Do I consider certain aspects of my professional life beneath me? Am I still trying to get inspired by the same old sources? Do I need to do something new? And you have to ask yourself one other thing, perhaps the most important thing of all: How do I define success?

Success isn't necessarily making a billion dollars. There are miserable billionaires and there are happy folks who work regular, nine-to-five jobs. Success is about being satisfied with your life and where it's heading, and that shouldn't mean the same thing to all of us. If professional success is important to you having a successful marriage or successful kids, that's fair. If what you value most is a life where most of your energy goes into the people you love, then to me, that's success. If you give your all to your job and you're making a contribution that is valuable and important, that's success—whether you're cash-checking or not. You don't have to be Diddy to be a success in my book. Just work hard at *something*. Love it and give it your best every day. That's what worked for me.

RULE #6:

Do Your Own Books

(But Read This One First)

Listening to some rap lyrics, you'd get the idea that once you have a little money, all you have to do is sit back, and watch it pile up. You'd get the idea that the hard part is in getting that first taste of the big bucks, but once you get it, the money grows on its own.

As I've said, I'm often asked to talk to young people and I hear the echo of this idea in the things they say.

Almost all of them have the ambition to be a baller or rap star. I'm not trying to discourage them, but I do think it's important to know the odds. If I talk to 1,000 kids, maybe one of them might actually get a music deal. If I talked to 10,000 of them, maybe one of them might have a hit. And that's it. One hit. The hope to be a multi-album success? You can count those people on one hand, because they are that rare. And we know their names because they have truly earned the distinction of "superstar." Your odds of that kind of success are literally one in millions. You should see the look on those kids faces when I hit them with that little bit of crushing reality. They wish I hadn't come to their school when I bring that happy bit of news.

Diddy and Michael Jordan are superstars because they've succeeded against incredible odds, but there's more. The super-successful musicians have also done some things that most of the one-hit wonders haven't done. The super-successful athletes have, too. They've kept up with their business affairs. They've hired the right advisors and monitored their work. They've reached beyond music and sports to capitalize on their talent in other ways. They've pursued acting, restaurants, clothing and liquor businesses. They've invested and taken risks. They've diversified. They fired all their "friends" years ago.

Knowing how to capitalize on your talents and how to invest the money you make from using them is the real lesson that these music and sports superstars can teach us. It's also Rule Number Six, if you're playing the game behind the game. I call it "do your own books," but when I say "do your books," I include the idea that it's your responsibility to make money, figure out how to spend it and have a strategy for making it grow. If you want to have money and keep it, trust no one, and I mean *no one*, else to manage it. Sure, you might need advisors but even then, your money is ultimately your responsibility and no one else's.

The best news is that you can learn how to count your money, how to invest it and how to do your own books without becoming a baller or rapper. You can learn how to make money grow even if you're working a minimum wage job. It doesn't take a lot of money to learn about money. It takes the time, energy and willingness to ask questions, do research and learn.

THE SECRET TO MAKING MONEY: QUIETLY SAVING

Everybody thinks you have to have a big chunk of money already before you can start doing things with it. That's the first mistake. The game behind the game plays money the opposite way. Stop thinking big and start thinking small. Stop thinking millions and start thinking about dollars. Or even just pennies.

Yeah, pennies.

You want to have money enough to count?

You have to start thinking about it differently. You have to start thinking about playing the wealth game for the long term, not just the short term. Being about a quick score of cash is nice for the few days the money lasts, but you'll be broke again faster than if you invest it all in your friends' crazy business ideas. As my father used to say, you put yourself in the position to win or fail. What you do with your pennies sets the stage for how you handle dollars.

Do you spend every single penny you make? If you do, you're not playing the game. You're not thinking long term. You're not setting the stage to invest in yourself.

Saving is the key to the game behind the game. If you can find a way to set a little cash aside, you're well on the way to cash-checking.

My father called himself a "quiet saver." That was his phrase for what he did with money. He didn't talk a lot about what he was doing with money; he kept his own financial house and minded his own financial business. He didn't see the need to inform others of his plans or his methods. He just continued to take small, daily actions to secure his financial future. It worked for him, so I've adopted it, too, because it works.

People often hated on my dad. They thought he was cheap and not generous. Both perceptions were totally incorrect. He would always give valuable investment information to people he thought really valued it and would use it wisely, but he refused to let people take advantage of him or his hard work. He once told me about how some of the haters would come up to him and say, "Tom, if you hear about a good deal let me know." To me, he'd say, "If I hear about a good deal I'm going to do it myself, G'damn it. Everybody wants something to drop in their laps. They want me to do their work." My father was right not to share. He did his due diligence. He wasn't about to give people who didn't appreciate it the information that he worked hard to obtain. I don't blame him, but that doesn't stop some people from expecting that others should give them something for nothing. We've talked about this before, in Rule Number Four—"Black-sphemy."

My father started his "quiet saver" plan while he was still in the Air Force. We lived well, but he never spent all that he had. He put some aside for a rainy day, or for a good opportunity. The opportunity came for him in the form of real estate, and he used the money he'd saved to buy small pieces of property. He rented them out and put a little more money aside until he had enough to buy more property.

He wasn't the ostentatious type—look it up, dammit (and don't name your son Ostentatious)—so people didn't know what he had. He wasn't one of those guys who wears his money, you know the type: loaded up with gold jewelry, diamond watches, thousand dollar jeans, the latest Italian shoes, silk shirt and the whole nine. You'll see that guy in the club ordering magnums of Cristal, then having to take the bus home and borrow money to get through the next two weeks until payday. He's all flash, but no substance. He wants to look like a player when in reality he doesn't have two nickels to rub together.

My father was the opposite. He wasn't cheap, but he understood how stupid it is to spend money on making *other people* think you have money. He understood how much smarter it is to *spend* money on getting *more money.* That's why people were surprised when it came time to buy a new car and my dad would drive off the lot in a fancy new Cadillac with all the bells and whistles. (Cars are the weakness he does have—and that I inherited.) They didn't know he had money like that. It wasn't his style to spend a lot of time and energy on impressing other people, but he was more than willing to spend his hard-earned cash on something he would really enjoy—like a nice car—as long as he didn't pay the sticker price!

Too many Black folks spend a lot of time *talking* about money and not much time actually doing anything with it. We spend our time complaining about how we need to get some money, about how hard it is to make some money and about how much things cost, but not much time learning how money works. We're not the ones going to those free investment seminars offered by financial experts. We don't have savings clubs with friends or family members like some cultures do, where everyone puts in a little bit from every paycheck for a year and at the end of the year, the money is used to invest in a joint venture, or given to one of the members to start a business. Finance websites aren't our homepages.

Yeah, I hear you grumbling,"Yeah, Russ Parr. We don't do that because we ain't got it like that. We don't got no extra money to be talking about investing. We're struggling just to survive here."

For some people, that's really true, but for many others it's a cop-out. Too many Black folks think cable TV and X-Box are life necessities. If you're serious about learning more about money, sell the X-Box and take some classes. Invest the money you spend on cable, movies and clubbing in figuring out a way to make that money grow.

Don't want to do that?

Then find other ways to make extra money, and save the money you earn. Too many people, especially young people, frown on taking on any kind of extra work that might give them a bit more financial freedom. Teenaged girls don't want to babysit anymore; teenaged boys don't shovel their neighbors walks or offer to cut the grass. Yeah, I know I sound like an old dude, but it's true. Many young people are unwilling to take jobs involving service, cleaning or the restaurant industry. Why? They don't want to get dirty.

Gaining financial independence means being willing to get dirty. It means doing the jobs no one wants to do until you have enough money set aside to do something else. Or it means learning things that are complicated, like how to invest in stocks or how to negotiate a contract. Or it means forgoing some "fun" things in order to quietly and carefully set money aside for a better purpose.

That's how the game of real wealth is played. No bullshit.

If you don't believe me, look at the people who have money. I'm not talking about actors and musicians and athletes now. I'm talking about your everyday people who are doing well and have achieved financial comfort and stability. They live within their means. They don't have debt. They aren't running out buying every new pair of sneakers and the latest phone just because they have to be the "first" to have it. Their spending isn't dictated by what Madison Avenue tells them it's "cool" to have. Instead, their spending, and saving, is dictated by their own goals and plans.

They don't buy to impress others or to achieve a

certain "look" or style (and by the way, most of you look a hot mess in some of that designer wear, but nobody will tell you the truth about it.) They don't spend emotionally. They spend intelligently. They do their own books. They're playing the game behind the game with their financial priorities, and the result is cash-checking.

SEEK OUT EXPERTS

"Go into business with a Jew."

I'll never forget when my father said that. It was the late 1960s, and I was about eleven years old. Of course, he was alluding to the old stereotypes about Jews and money. Those ideas are not politically correct now, but they were the kinds of things that were commonly said in that time. Remember, this is the same guy who used to put up with nigger jokes on the golf course.

You don't need to resort to stereotypes to find out who knows what you need to know. My father didn't have Yahoo! Finance™ to help him find out who knew what he needed to know, or where to get the kinds of information he needed. You *do* have the Internet, so really there's no excuse.

As I've said before, the Internet offers all of us whole new ways to find out things we don't know. It's a matter of choosing to abandon all the many responsibilities of your Farmville animals for the thrills of The Street.com instead. It's a matter of skipping TMZ or Media Take Out for one of the many blogs on managing money, buying properties or setting up a business.

It doesn't matter to me whether you play the stock market or invest in real estate like my father did. You can be researching how to create a game application to sell to Apple™. Instead of always being the consumer, you can become a creator. Content is King. That's cash-checking. Instead of spending all your time on celebrity blog sites bullshitting, why not start your own? Work on getting a following and attracting advertising. Work with what interests you, with what you know. If the local clubs are your thing, figure out how to share information on them with the people who follow that kind of thing. How do you make your information the best—so good that people want to pay for it? That kind of research, dedication and expertise is what leads to cash-checking. There are resources everywhere for any kind of venture you can imagine, if you're willing to invest the time and attention on finding out about them. While you don't have to do what my father did, or use the kinds of ugly stereotypes that were part of his generation, it never hurts to "make nice" with people who know more than you do. I am not a financial expert by any means, but I'm very good at calling on people who know more than me.

Consider it a corollary to Rule Number Three to make people who *know things* love you. Corollary? Look it up. (I just pulled that word out of my ass, but I think it's the right one!) I keep telling you to look up stuff so you can get into the habit of researching vital information that you may need to get that money. Even if you don't know what a "corollary" is, you should know that finding a mentor who is an expert in the field or industry you're interested in is the move. Use the strategy of Rule Number Three to get taken under that more experienced person's wing. Being loved—or at least liked—by a person who is already successful in a specific business makes it easier to learn about that business. Rules One and Three apply here. You have to earn the person's trust, and you can't expect to do that with some insincere bullshit or some fan-turned-stalker mess. You're going to have to find something legitimate and real to offer (like a bag of good weed . . . just kidding) or at least something that sounds that way. Building a relationship with someone who knows what you need to know is one of the best ways to get to cash-checking, as long as you understand that you still have to follow Rule Number Five. You still have to do the hard work it's going to take to get you where you need to be. Other people may share their knowledge, but they are not going to do it for you.

By the way, this suggestion will not work on me. Please do not try to be my friend to break into radio. I have a doctorate in bullshit and I can smell you.

INVESTING IN YOUR TALENTS—AND IN THE TALENTS OF OTHERS

I can't tell you how many times I've talked with young people who want to go into the music business, but who haven't even put up a video of themselves singing or rapping or whatever on YouTube. You say "let's hear it," and they don't have a CD, they don't have an MP3 to email you, and they don't even have a little clip of themselves on their I-Phone. They are completely unprepared, but every other word they say is "put me on blast" and "blow me up."

How is anyone supposed to help you if you haven't helped yourself? How can you encourage others to invest in you if you haven't been willing to invest in yourself? Talents *are* cash. They are cash opportunities waiting to be converted. If you don't take the time to invest in your talents by honing them, by working on them and developing them, and by committing your own money to them, you can't be mad. By the way, do not ask a good friend or your grandma to confirm how talented you are. These are not objective sources. They are not going to be honest. Even if you can't sing a lick, your Granny will tell you how great you sound. Take her point of view with a grain of salt. Grandma's *lie.*

By the time I was a junior or so in high school, I knew I was interested in radio. My family was living in California and there was a small Black-owned radio station a couple of towns away. The DJ was this older dude named "Mr. D," and he was willing to let me sell some advertising time in exchange for my own show. I hit the streets and sold advertising to many liquor stores, laundromats, etc. until I had enough money to get on the radio, and that's how "Dr. RDP," my first radio persona and the host of my first show, was born. I did that for almost a year. It was an incredible learning experience and a lot of fun, too.

It also ended up helping me get my first job in radio at KABC. I told you about that already. It was a good thing that I had invested the time and money to learn something about radio when I was a teenager.

"Yeah, Russ Parr," you're saying. "But not everybody's had your chances. And not everybody's got your ability to bullshit their way in the door."

True, but everybody can find ways to invest in their interests. Not every way involves money. Sometimes the investment is in time. Sometimes the investment is paid for in your labor. Sometimes you invest with your willingness to practice. Sometimes the investment comes in being willing to give up other things to pursue something you hope will lead to cash-checking. Discipline is required to develop any talent. It's as important as any financial investment. I didn't get paid to do my first radio program. I had to sell advertising to get the chance. Sometimes you have to work for free to get through the door.

For the record, my father wasn't the sort who just "gave me" money. He was willing to help me, but only up to a point. While he was willing to invest a certain amount of what he had acquired in his life in me, he also left me with the responsibility of contributing to my own success. That's why I had to resort to taking money out of his wallet while he was sleeping! (Just kidding, again.) Seriously, I had to invest my own time and money before he'd invest a dime of his.

Another thing my dad has always said is that it is a smart business move to use other people's money for your ventures when you can, even if it's your dad's. For example, around the same time I started that first radio show, back in junior college, I got interested in DJ-ing. This was the late 1970s, and I used to spend hours with our old stereo system trying to mix records and create sounds. I spent so much time doing that that finally my father bought me some equipment: a couple of turntables and an amplifier, I think, along with a decent microphone. The tools of the trade of party DJ.

"Okay," he said. "Here are your tools. Go get some business. Turn this music you're interested in into something you can make some money off of. When you do, you can pay me back for the tools."

I did. I started advertising myself as a DJ and doing parties and things. I used his financial investment in materials and added to it my own investment, in time, to let people know what I could do. I made money, then I paid him back. I made more money, and I invested it in my radio show.

That's how it works. I spent the time learning how to spin records—so much time that my father thought I might be serious enough about it to justify his financial investment. I took his financial investment and used it to both gain more experience and to repay him.

These steps—interest, investment, opportunity, re-investment, followed by more opportunity—will work with almost endeavor, field or interest you might have. Don't tell me you don't have any money—it's usually not required to start. If you're willing to spend the time and make some sacrifices to get something better than what you have, somehow the money will come. There was a time when I had to do things I wasn't proud of, like male exotic dancing. I had this ripped body, so I made money dancing at Bat Mitzvahs (teenaged Jewish girls just love to celebrate coming of age by hiring a Black stripper) and in nightclubs. I soon realized I was just spinning my wheels because the tips weren't big enough to justify prostituting myself. Besides, I really wasn't a good dancer. I didn't figure out that I was putting my G-string on backwards for six months. The sad part is that no one *else* noticed I was wearing the G-string backwards!

Okay, that never happened. It might have happened, and I would have done it if I didn't have this belly on me, but since I have the belly, it never happened. Erase.

MIND YOUR MONEY

The same young kids who dream big dreams about big money without having any kind of plan for actually achieving that lofty financial status are often the ones who think that they'll have "people" who will safely and effectively manage their funds while they simply enjoy spending.

This is bullshit, and once again, not the useful kind. In fact, expecting other people to manage your money for you is a good way to lose every cent you ever made. If you're playing the game behind the game, you mind your own money and you know what's on your books.

Think of it this way: once you're cash-checking, you have all of your old responsibilities about making money plus a couple of new ones. The number one responsibility you have to your money, whether you have a lot or little, is to manage it yourself. You need to do your own books, and if you become successful enough to need others to help you with your assets, you need to know at least enough about where your assets are and what they're supposed to be doing to tell if those people are cheating you.

This is yet another financial lesson I learned from my father at young age. I used to sit behind him while he did his own books. He had one of those old green ledgers with the double columns. You wrote down incoming money on one side and expenses on the other. I remember watching him enter the figures and not understanding what he was doing at all.

"See, I got this here and that there," he'd say and he'd start to get excited. I didn't understand it then, but I do now: watching your money pile up *is* exciting. The more I watched him, the better I understood just how he accounted for the rents and expenses of managing his real estate ventures. I understood it even better when I was a young father and in college and he sent me out to manage one of his buildings. I got to understand firsthand the expenses of managing a building and how hard it can be to deal with tenants and collect what it is owed you. It was a powerful lesson because, while I knew my father owned properties, I had no idea how much work was involved in maintaining them.

"He owns all them properties," some people might have said about my dad. "He got that building. He's rich."

It does sound impressive: owning a building, but I can tell you, having tried to manage one, and having been responsible for collecting the rent and making sure that everything inside was in working order, it's a lot of work.

It's easy to hate on someone for having things, especially when you don't know about all the crap they had to go through to get there. It's easy to mutter under your breath about someone when you don't know how hard they are still working just to stay where they are. The more you "get" in this life, the greater the responsibility you have to learn about it, to keep up with it, and to stay on top of the people around you who are supposed to be working for you. That's not easy.

If you're going to play the game behind the game, keeping up with money is going to become a bigger and bigger part of your life. You're going to have to understand where it is, what it's doing and what's supposed to be happening to it. You're going to have to understand ledgers, expenses and assets. You're going to have to know your own books. If you have to delegate to someone who knows more than you, make sure you do your homework and ask questions. If you don't, you should just bend over. You *will* get screwed.

I know this from personal experience.

Back when I had the group, *Bobby Jimmy and the Critters,* I had a manager named Jerry Heller. This was the mid-1980s—like 1986 or 1987—and "We Like Ugly Women" and "Roaches" had been pretty successful hip hop hits. I met Jerry Heller through Don McMillan, who owned Macola Records, the company that distributed our records. Jerry was smart—smart enough to see an opening in the burgeoning hip hop culture growing in LA. He knew enough to take advantage of an opportunity when he met one, and pretty soon, he was managing me and the groups from my record label, Rapsur Records. I ended up introducing him to NWA's Eazy E (the late Eric Wright) and the LA Dream Team and all those guys that I used to make music with back in the day. Jerry ended up representing all of us. He was actually a pretty cool guy in lots of ways. He was an older Jewish guy with white hair, and he used to go into the 'hoods of LA with us, and hang out.

He liked us, but that didn't stop him from screwing us, financially. Or at least, that's what I believed for a long time. In hindsight, he never really screwed us. He told us what he was going to do with the money he collected on our behalf. He just knew we weren't business savvy enough to ask the right questions about why he was doing it or whether that was fair. So, as much as I'd like to say he screwed us, I guess I'll have to give him a pass on that.

Instead, I'll say this: Jerry Heller was working the rules. He was using his ability to bullshit to take care of what he needed to keep *his* business growing. He worked the strategy like a master. He took the time to get to know us and our interests and to get us to love him. He was charming and charismatic. He also was hard working and developed an area of expertise in music representation that I didn't have. He knew more than I did and I needed him to get the groups out there and to get us gigs. At first, everything was fine. Jerry was helping us to make money and was making money off us. At some point, I started to get a little suspicious. I got suspicious because I finally started asking the right questions.

Questions are the key. I have nothing against getting expert help. In fact, I recommend it. If you're going to set up a business, if you're going to acquire property, if you're going to hire people or doing anything that involves serious cash-checking, you're going to need the advice of people who know more than you do. At some point, you really will need a lawyer or an accountant, or an agent or some other kind of management or expertise. You'll need to research that person as thoroughly and as carefully as any other decision you make. That's a part of your responsibility as the client—to research who you choose to represent you or to assist you. The other part of your job as the client is to get as educated as you can. Make sure you're an expert on your *own* money. Later on, Ice Cube (who was a member of NWA) would leave the group for some of the same reasons that I parted ways with Heller. Cube was (and still is) a highly intelligent street dude. Heller didn't anticipate that Cube would have the knowledge or savvy to challenge the business agenda that was lining Jerry's pockets. Heller aligned himself with Eazy E, NWA's leader, but unfortunately Eazy E, talented as he was, wasn't the real star of NWA. That was Ice Cube. Heller put enough money in Eazy's pocket to convince him that he didn't need Cube and, of course, the rest is history.

Some people are great at asking questions when it comes to things like buying cars and shopping in stores. I remember my father used to say "never pay full price" and he didn't. One of his favorite things to do on a Saturday afternoon was go to a car dealership and play games with the salesmen. We'd walk in and there would be one price. We'd hesitate, and there'd be another price. We'd head for the parking lot to leave, and the price would change again. "Never take the first price," he told me. And I don't. The other thing I learned from him in those experiences is that if someone's going to be making money off me, or if I'm going to be spending money on their services, then I have the right to ask questions—as many questions as I want. If I don't get the answers I want, I walk out and take my business elsewhere.

Treat advisors like any other major purchase and ask questions. Ask questions. Ask questions.

Ask questions and keep asking them until you understand exactly what it is the people you hire are going to do and how they're going to do it. The thing about a bad advisor is that eventually, they will give you just enough information for you to realize that they are screwing you!

That's what happened with good old Jerry Heller. I

kept asking him about our royalties and about our gigs and he'd start talking and talking and the stories didn't go together. Remember, this is a critical part of Rule Number One: "Remember Your Bullshit." I told you about how dangerous it can be to forget your bullshit, because then you have to bullshit on your bullshit? Keep your stories straight because having to bullshit on your bullshit increases the likelihood that you're going to get caught bullshitting.

Poor old Jerry didn't keep his stories straight. He started to compound his bullshit daily, and he got caught. Get your yellow highlighter pen out and take note. First, there's "bullshit," which we've already defined. Second, there's the "bullshitter." This is the person that is spewing partial truths and factual embellishments. Finally, there's the "bullshit-ee." This is the person who is receiving the bullshit. Are you following me here? Good, because this is the important part: You never want to be the bullshit-ee. That's what I was with the legendary Jerry Heller.

I know you've heard the sad stories of so many professional athletes, actors and musicians who entrusted their business affairs to others and ended up right back at broke. Or even worse, ended up even more broke than they started because they *owed* so many people money after their brief flirtation with fame and fortune. The truth of that situation is that at least part of their fate was their own fault for trusting that *anyone else* will look out for your money as well as *you* do. At least part of their fate is their own fault because they didn't ask enough questions or the right questions. They didn't ask to see the books, and they didn't take the time to do the research and find out about the people who were supposed to be looking out for them.

Ask questions. Read your contracts before you sign them. Make the people you hire prove their trustworthiness, and once it's proven, reward them with your continued business. Even then, review your own books. Cash-checking means exactly that—it's up to you to check on your cash, to invest it and to make it grow.

Just in case you missed it earlier, take a tip from the superstars: Don't hire your friends!

RULE #7:

Don't Recommend Dumbass Motherf#%^ers

We're halfway through my rules for cash-checking and succeeding in the game behind the game, so I figured I'd give you a break. This will be a really short rule. It will be easy to read and easy to remember. Here it is:

Don't recommend any dumb motherf#%^ers. They'll just make you look bad. If you look bad because of some dumb motherf#%^er, you hurt your own game.

That's it.

Told you it was a short rule.

Turn the page.

RULE #8:

Find Your Gut . . .

(Or Do Some Crunches)

Some of the prior rules might have you thinking that, to play the game behind the game, you have to be always thinking, always plotting like some kind of mad scientist or evil villain in your secret lab.

"Haha! If they do *this*, then I'll do *that!*" Rub your hands together maniacally. "And when they do *this,* I'll have them in my power! HAHAHAH!"

Not quite.

While cash-checking and SWB (succeeding while Black, remember?) do involve their fair share of thought, the game does indeed have a heart. Or at least a stomach. Much of what I've learned about SWB involves trust, but not my eyes and ears, or even my intellectual analysis of what appears to be happening in a particular situation. Instead, success comes down to finding your gut and trusting it.

FINDING YOUR GUT

No, I don't mean your abs, though some of you probably need to do that, too. They should be somewhere between your neck and your groin area, and if you don't feel a six-pack, I recommend a few crunches. Maybe more than a few—and few less six packs of the alcoholic kind, perhaps?

Seriously, when I say "gut," I mean something else. I mean knowing how to access that part of you that knows without knowing. Some people call that their "heart," but I'm hesitant to use that word. "Heart" is also the center for emotion, and I'm not talking about making emotional decisions. In fact, if there's one thing that I think you have to avoid if you're going to succeed while black, it's making decisions based on any emotion. Rather, decisions have to made on gut. "Gut" sounds better than "nuts," so let's go with it.

"Gut" to me is almost a formula. It's head + heart + long term goal + the realities of the circumstances. A gut decision isn't something that can be made in advance, and it isn't something that anyone else can advise you of. It really is a decision that feels right in your body. It's a decision that has a logic all its own.

Too many people make their decisions based on what their friends say or what they think other people want them to do. That's a good way to be just like everybody else. If you aspire to cash-checking, you're going to have to leave what your friends say behind you. Following your gut can be a lonely road, but I promise you, if you can do it, it brings life's best rewards.

YOU'RE CRAZY, MAN

When I left Los Angeles for Dallas in 1989, to many of the people in my life it probably seemed like a crazy decision. I had been doing well in Los Angeles. I had been successful on television with *Rock 'N' America*, and I had been successful in music with my own record label with several groups including *Bobby Jimmy and the Critters*. I had regular appearances doing stand-up, and had had some success on the radio. I had friends, family and relationships in the industry that made staying in LA seem like a smart decision.

But my gut told me to leave.

My gut and the $100,000 salary the Texas station was offering me to take over their drive-time morning show, and that was in 1989 dollars. Up until that point in my career, I'd never had a six-figure salary, and even though I had lots of projects in the works, a steady income in that range looked pretty damn good. I did make money off of *Bobby Jimmy*, but the idea of a salary was still appealing.

But good as the salary was, there were some serious disadvantages to making the move to Dallas.

The first one was Tom Joyner.

"You're crazy." That's what a lot of my friends and business associates said when I told them I had to decided to go to Dallas and compete head to head with Tom Joyner's wildly popular radio show. "You're going to get eaten alive. It's going to ruin your career."

I took it as a challenge. After all, I was used to working hard, and I thought I was pretty funny. Beating Tom in his home market would be a tremendous accomplishment, and I thought I could do it.

"What about your other projects?" my friends asked.

It was true, it might be more difficult to pursue standup or my music from Dallas, but not impossible, I decided. After all, I was talking about moving to Texas, not the furthest reaches of Outer Mongolia.

Even if I *had* been moving to the furthest reaches of Outer Mongolia I probably still would have left. Why?

Did I mention the $100,000?

But it wasn't just that. My gut was telling me that I needed to make this move, and not just for the money.

My gut told me that my life in Los Angeles, for all of the good things that were happening, wasn't moving in the direction that I truly wanted. Intellectually things looked good, but just below the surface was a feeling that, as time went on, I would find the things I was doing less fulfilling than if I continued to do to my first love—radio—and tried to use my talent for it to its full advantage. Then, there was the atmosphere in Los Angeles to consider. Around that time in LA, cops were choking brothers out. People think of California as "liberal," but at that time, Los Angeles was a very conservative city and things were starting to happen that made me nervous.

I bought a new car—well, not completely new. It was a used BMW. The people at the dealership said, "Hey, it's okay to take the license plate from the car you're turning in and put it on the BMW." So I did it. I'm rolling down Sunset Boulevard, enjoying life. In my review mirror I notice all these cop cars with their lights flashing and their sirens wailing. I could see a helicopter through my sun roof. I said to myself, "Somebody is about to get fucked up."

I never thought it might be me. During this time I was riding high. I had a national McDonald's commercial on TV. I was the "Big Mac Man." It ran so much that people actually recognized me as the guy from the commercial. The next thing I know, I'm on the ground surrounded by at least 20 LAPD being called a "nigger" by a Mexican cop with a shotgun pointed at my head. They thought I stole the car because the license plate on the vehicle didn't match up with the make and model on file with the DMV. You see, driving while Black (DWB) in LA was frowned upon, especially in a nice upscale vehicle like a BMW.

I was scared to death. I remember hearing a little girl say, "Mommy, isn't that the Big Mac Man?" as a crowd formed. It was terrible. After that experience, leaving LA wasn't a totally emotion-free decision. I decided to move.

As I've explained in Rule Number Three—"Make People Love You," the move was difficult. It was culture shock for me, as an African American who had lived the majority of his life on the west coast, to adapt to and adopt a different idea way of experiencing blackness. I already shared with you the difficulty that I had in finding my footing with humor and making my new audience like me. I'll add that I often felt personally isolated, since I really didn't know anyone and had left all my friends behind in Los Angeles.

I had also left a girlfriend in Los Angeles. With no disrespect to her, leaving her behind turned out to be a good thing because I met Darnell, the woman who would become my wife, in Dallas. We've been married now for twenty years and have three children together. She changed the shape and direction of my life, my career and probably saved my life.

I like to think my "gut" feelings about leaving Los Angeles for the new and unknown potential in Dallas was actually a decision that recognized something my conscious mind did not: That I needed a life partner who would be able to help me build the brand that would become the *Russ Parr Morning Show.* My gut knew that I wouldn't meet that person in Los Angeles. My gut knew that she was in Dallas. I'd be lying if I said I knew that when I left LA, but I did know that I was missing something important in Los Angeles. I had to leave to find out just what that was.

LOVE AT FIRST SIGHT

The reason you should trust your gut is because your gut is smarter than you will ever be. It takes the information that you receive with your eyes and your ears, your heart and brain and connects them to the Great Unknown. You can call that God or the Universe or whatever you want. Black people usually call that power "Jesus" or "Allah," but the longer I live, the more I believe "gut" may indeed be another word for "God."

I was at a club, working, not socializing. I was doing a live remote at a place called RJ's By the Lake. This beautiful woman came over to me and said, "I like what you said on the radio." She had heard the emotional story I recounted about a teenage girl who was being molested by her mom's boyfriend. The little girl was scared. The abuser had threatened to kill her if she told, but when she discovered she was pregnant by this dude, she finally told her mom. Her mom confronted the abuser and demanded abortion money. The dude went ballistic and wound up killing almost everybody in the family. In the radio broadcast, I had told the story as justification for my support of the death penalty. My wife later said that it was the first time she heard me being serious on the radio, and that she had been impressed by it.

Did I mention that she was (and still is) beautiful? But it wasn't just that. It was her words. I was constantly working to build a fan base in Dallas, and encouragement was hard to come by. Getting that kind of feedback from someone like Darnell (did I mention how beautiful she was—and still is?) meant a lot to me.

I think I was in love with her immediately. I knew she was the one for me almost from that very first instant, from the way she spoke and the conversation we had. I thought I had been in love with other people before, but this was different. There was no reason for why I loved her—and every reason. She was smart and sharp and insightful and didn't put up with any crap. She was, and is, the exact balance to my personality that I hadn't known that I was looking for until she was standing right in front of me.

I have always been a pleaser; I've always tried to make people happy and keep the peace. In my relationships with women, that tendency had put me in situations where I'd sometimes felt like I was being used or taken advantage of. One of my weaknesses is that I'll fall for any sad story. It's a weakness in my game, but an even greater weakness in my personal relationships. There are plenty of women out there who can see guys like me coming, and are ready and willing to milk us for all we're worth. My mom is the one who gave me that "sucker" gene, only she wore it better. While I'm a sucker, she was "compassionate." I guess you could call me compassionate, too, because I care about people, too. I really do. My friends get all that loyalty, all that helpfulness and blind concern.

That's why I don't have many friends.

My relationship with my son's mother hadn't worked out. His mother and I married the day I graduated from college, just as I promised her, but there were problems the whole time and the marriage lasted only a year and a half before we separated. It took us years to divorce. I stayed legally married out of guilt and the fear that if I did anything that upset the apple cart, my son's mother would make it difficult for me to see and be with my son.

Until Darnell.

My gut told me that Darnell was different. I was smart enough to turn off my brain and listen to it. It was right.

She was married to someone else at the time, but that relationship was already in distress. I knew I wanted to be with her, but I also knew I had to wait until the time was right. We were married after we both severed our relationships legally.

Because she's the right partner for me, she enhances my game and has been an indispensable asset in my quest to succeed while Black. My wife balances me. She offers a completely different approach to the game. She's tough. Sometimes, my strategies get all tangled up in my head. It's then when she's an invaluable advisor. She's like, "No. These people don't appreciate you. Fuck 'em."

Thanks, baby. I needed that. Of course, if she divorces me after this book comes out, I'll take back everything I've just said about her.

A GUT IN THE GAME

Yes, I know. You're saying, "Russ, this was supposed to be a how to handle your business book. This book is supposed to be about making money. About cash-checking, man. What you getting all mushy for?"

Three reasons.

First, your career doesn't exist in a vacuum. Many of us work hard to provide for the people in our lives that we care about—whoever they are. Having a supportive partner is a tremendous asset to your professional life, just as being in a bad relationship can be a huge drain on your career success. It's all in the energy. When your personal life is good and you have harmony in your home, you have extra energy to bring to your professional game. Personal strife, on the other hand, sucks energy.

Darnell's support allows me to ramp up the energy I bring to the workplace. Having her as a sounding board gives me additional ideas and strategies to bring to SWB. That is an incredible advantage, and you know I'm right because you know, like I do, how many people bring their personal drama into the workplace and let it distract them from getting the job done.

In my movie *The Last Stand*, one of the comedians gets the opportunity to be in a movie. He's got a very small part, just one line, really, but it doesn't matter. It's a big break for him and is the kind of chance that might let him finally leave behind working multiple minimum wage jobs and begin his career as a working actor. Unfortunately, his wife keeps calling . . . and calling . . . and calling, interrupting the action on the movie set and driving everyone crazy because she's jealous and thinks her man is cheating on her. She calls so many times that what should have been a simple scene stretches over hours.

She calls so much the director gets pissed off and fires the guy.

Now, obviously, in *The Last Stand*, the situation was written to be dramatic, but in every day workplaces, these kinds of situations play out daily. Sometimes personal dramas do lead to terminations. More often, they lead to wasted time and to gossip. They change the way you are perceived in the work environment. After all, if you can't manage your personal affairs, you're not going to be perceived as someone who is capable of taking on greater responsibilities on the job. It won't matter how great you are at bullshitting, how hard you work or how many people like you, if you're constantly on the phone with your girl or your boy or your kids or your mother, you've got a problem. The whole game goes down the drain if your personal life overtakes your professional life. There's nothing worse than having your girl show up at your job and threaten to whup the ass of any woman she catches looking at her man. It makes you look weak. It makes you look like an idiot.

The second reason is that, even if you keep your private affairs private for the most part, when things aren't going well, your productivity is affected. So, even if you're not fielding constant phone calls or having to "duck out" for a few minutes to handle your personal business, chances are pretty good you won't have as much to give your job if you're dealing with a lot of drama outside of it. Having a solid, drama free relationship helps on that level, too.

The third reason that I've spent so much time telling you about my wife in this chapter—and in this book about being in the business game—is that she is my best advisor. She represents how I select my advisors—and make some my biggest professional moves. I trusted my gut when I moved to Dallas, and I trusted my gut when I met Darnell, and in both cases, my gut was right.

In professional settings you need to determine who to trust. Who will be a good mentor? Who can be trusted? Who is an enemy? Who is an ally? While I believe in getting your Google™ on (doing the research) and I've said it many times, I also believe in a power beyond thinking. Being in touch with that power leads to the best decisions, both about what to do and who to trust. I believe in making decisions based on your gut. Your gut is part of your game, and the better you are at finding it, reading it and acting on its guidance, the further you're likely to go.

And don't forget those crunches, either!

RULE #9:

Let Other People *Think* They Win

(When It's Okay to Be a Loser)

You're sitting in a meeting. Everyone's looking for a solution to a problem and you've had a brainstorm.

"Hey, everyone, let's try this!" You say.

Your boss shakes her head. "No, that won't work."

The meeting continues. Other ideas are suggested and all of them are shot down.

"I know," Boss Lady says at last. "What we should do is . . ." and she proceeds to share with the group the exact brainstorm idea that you suggested fifteen minutes before.

All heads swing to you. Everyone in the room heard you offer the exact same suggestion only minutes before. It's the moment of truth. Do you:

(a) Become indignant and say, "But that's what I said fifteen minutes ago! Bitch trying to steal my idea!"
(b) Roll your eyes, but say nothing.
(c) Nod enthusiastically and say, "What a great idea!"
(d) Suggest another idea that's better than the first one.
(e) None of the above.

This is a test. It's a pop quiz to see if you are paying attention to what I've been trying to teach you here. Do you remember the name of this rule, because if you do, you know that the correct is:

(c).

Yes, (c). Yes, the boss just stole your idea and yes, your response is to be the biggest cheerleader to ever shake a pom-pom. Your job here is to let the boss win, or at least let it *appear* that the boss has won. The answer is (c) because the boss is the boss, of course, and cussing the boss out is always a losing idea. The answer isn't (d) because even if you have a better idea, one-upping the boss is also always a losing idea. And the answer isn't (b) because communicating disdain for the boss is a losing idea. There can only really be one answer that keeps the bullshit alive and follows the rules of the game behind the game.

I'm an opposite kind of guy. If you thought I'd suggest you try to take some action to "assert yourself" or "take down the boss," you really haven't been paying attention.

When someone has control of your paycheck, *let them win*. Smile when they steal your idea! You have reason to smile. By supporting the boss—by letting him or her know that you care about making him or her look good—you are securing your own future. Who will be asked to lead this project or implement this solution in the workplace? You. Who will be the boss's go-to guy or girl on this issue? You. Who will be the one kicked upstairs by her superiors? Okay, that will be Boss Lady, but who will she recommend take her position?

You.

Making the boss look good makes you look good. That's a rule of the game that has been a key component of the Old Boy Network for decades. It's something that White kids learn from the first employment experience, and something that seems to offend many young Black kids' sense of fairness.

"You kissin' the Man's ass, Russ Parr," these high school students say when I'm invited to speak. "You kissin' ass . . . Yo, nice car."

Get this, young heads: the world of work isn't fair. It's a game that has rules that may seem wrong to you. It has rules that sometimes seem to reward people who are as dumb as onions, but if you understand them, those rules will also reward *you*, too.

If you are younger than 40, it's not completely your fault if you don't understand the game. You were born in the 1970s and raised in a generation that was taught, "You gotta come at me with some respect." What you haven't been taught is this: that attitude buys little when you're working toward cash-checking.

Bosses appreciate loyalty. They appreciate employees who seem to want to help them get ahead. They appreciate employees who aren't threatened and who let them win. The smart employee understands that it just makes *sense* to let the boss win almost all of the time. The only exceptions are when the boss wants to win on something immoral or illegal—and those situations should be pretty obvious. In almost every other case, it's going to be in your interest to let the boss win, especially if you are still working your other strategies to either get to the place where *you're* the boss or you hope to use the boss to get to your next (and better) position.

What if one of your co-workers is the offending party, sitting up in that meeting, stealing your bullshit? Is it okay to shout out, "Bitch stole my idea!" when your co-worker steals your idea and sells it to the boss, taking your credit? If one of your co-workers—an equal, not a superior—steals your idea doesn't that give you the right to go off?

Not really. Let him win . . . and you'll still win.

Remember as a kid we used to say "cheaters never win?" They don't. And in this case, I'd bet your thieving co-worker won't have the skills to implement your brilliant idea. Losing gracefully in the meeting—and letting them take the credit and the lead—will more than likely mean that co-worker's shortcomings will be revealed sooner rather than later. People who like the thrill of getting credit for other people's work rarely like the hard work that goes along with implementing someone else's ideas.

"Great idea!" you say to that co-worker and you sit back and let them take charge. You sit back and watch them fail. I don't mean that in a malicious way, but it is true. Cheaters never win. Cheaters can't stop people with real ideas. If they're decent bullshitters, they'll be able to fake it for a while, but only for a while. If you're working all the other rules, you've got nothing to worry about. You can take the loss, let your co-worker think he or she is winning and still come out on top in the end.

Not to mention, your calm is going to completely freak them out. They'll be expecting a fight, and when they don't get it, it's going to leave them rattled, guilty and watching their back. Karma is bitch and she's going to be gunning for that idea stealer like nobody's business!

BIGGER LOSSES

Sometimes, however, no matter how hard you work, no matter how well you bullshit, no matter how much people like you and no matter how much you anticipate every possible negative, you will lose. No one is always a winner. Everyone loses out sometimes, and you will not be the exception.

Losing is part of the game behind the game. It's part of *every* game.

Sometimes, you will get passed over for promotion.

Sometimes, someone will steal your idea, make it work and get all the glory.

Sometimes, your boss won't remember that the idea was yours.

Sometimes you will get stabbed in the back.

Sometimes you will get betrayed.

It happens to everyone and it will happen to you.

I told you earlier about my stand up career. Joke swipers constantly stole from me and others. Back in the mid 80s, when I working at 1580 KDAY in LA, there was a TV show on called "Solid Gold" hosted by Arsenio Hall. Those writers and producers were shameless. They would literally rip my concepts and bits off from my radio broadcasts and reenact them on TV. Now, before I get accused of hatin' on Arsenio, let me say that he wasn't writing the show. He probably didn't have a thing to do with it, and at first I was flattered. I mean, I must be a pretty funny guy to have these TV people ripping off whole bits and putting them on a popular national TV show. It was cool. Then, I started to notice a pattern. When I moved to Dallas and produced *Flava TV,* some of the comedy skits we did showed up on the Wayans Brothers show *In Living Color*. Yeah, you can say "great writers think alike," but when they used the same punch lines *and* the characters names? Come on people! Steal if you must, but at least change the names of the characters! That sort of laziness is egregious! (Look it up, and don't name your son Egregious and start telling people it's the name of a Greek God! Don't bullshit if it's verifiable, that's Rule Number One!)

I would go to radio conventions and listen to airchecks of other radio personalities and hear my own material. I'm Mr. Opposite, so instead of confronting them, I would go and joke with the offenders. "If you need more material, I'm gonna have some brand new stuff Monday morning!" I'd say. "Help yourself!"

I love fucking with people, especially people who know they're wrong and are expecting to be on the receiving end of my anger. Letting them think they've won hasn't hurt me at all. I'm bigger than that, and by not saying a word, I prove it. Letting other people think they've gotten away with something is smart game play, and it works in all kinds of other situations, too.

STRATEGIC BULLSHIT FOR EVERY DAY USE: DO THE OPPOSITE

Letting other people think they've won has all kinds of practical uses, especially when people get confrontational. Do the opposite of what they expectand you can turn the whole dynamic to your favor. Don't believe me? Here are few true stories from my everyday life that prove the point. In these examples, embellishment wasn't required. This is exactly what happened—no bullshit!

I was going through the drive-through teller lane of my local bank. I pulled up and reached out to grab that little box thingy to insert my paperwork, when I realized I hadn't actually *done* the paperwork yet. So I got out my checkbook and my pen and started to work.

A horn blares from behind me and an old White man rolls down his window to scream out, "You're supposed to do the paperwork *before* you get in the line, you stupid motherfucker!"

Of course, instinctively I wanted to get out of the car and fuck this dude up, but I'm so used to responding to life's difficult situations with bullshit that Mr. Opposite kicked in. I decided to try something else altogether.

Now, I'm gonna tell you the truth: I don't really know the Bible well enough to quote it chapter and verse, so those of you who do, don't get mad at me for getting this all wrong. I've already admitted that a lot of what comes out of my mouth is bullshit, so don't hate.

"Sir," I said to him, my most humble and Christ-like voice. "As it is written in Matthew, chapter 4, verse 13, 'Be kind to your fellow man. Love your neighbor.' So sir, I say God bless you. God bless you, sir, today and all the days of your life."

And I finished my transaction.

I was about to pull off when that guy got out of his car and walked up to my window. "I'm sorry," he said. "I'm very, very sorry."

I just sat there and watched while the tears rolled down his cheeks. Then I drove away.

I do shit like that all the time just to *fuck* with people. It works because it robs them of the response they thought they were going to get. Some people walk around expecting a confrontation, just begging for one. Not giving it to them completely disarms them.

Now here's another one from the practical application of the rules of bullshit file. Always, always, always *let the cops win.*

I was driving with my sons in downtown DC and was a little turned around in getting where I wanted to be. The road I wanted to take was barricaded, but I didn't see that as a big obstacle. I proceeded through it and the sirens blasted out almost immediately.

The cop jumped out of his car and started screaming and yelling at me. I looked at my boys in the backseat and I could tell they were mortified. They were watching me, wondering how I was going to handle this man screaming in my face. And yeah, I was getting angry, but I also knew this was one of those situations where the smartest thing to do was push my real feelings to the side and let the bullshit flow free.

"What the hell did you think you were doing?" the officer yelled. "Didn't you see the cones? You're not supposed to go that way! It's clearly marked!"

"You're right officer," I said meekly. "I deserve this ticket."

"You're not supposed to go through when it's barricaded!" He kept screaming like I was an idiot.

"You're right, officer. I deserve the ticket."

"Get out of the car! Stand over there!"

"Okay."

I stood where he wanted and did what he wanted. Finally, when he didn't have any other basis to hold me and nothing left to yell at me for, he gave me my ticket and drove away.

I got back in the car.

"Dad, why'd you let him talk to you like that?" My boys were all big eyes and questions. They were bugged to see their dad—a six-foot-two inch, two hundred fifty pound Black man—being disrespected.

"Because," I answered truthfully, "That guy would like nothing better than to arrest me with you guys in the car. He'd like nothing better than to take me to jail in front of you, and I wasn't going to give him that. I'm glad you saw that because there are times for confrontation, and there's time when there's nothing to be gained. He took one look at me and he was expecting a confrontation, and I gave him the opposite." Let's also not forget that he has a gun.

Letting the cops win is playing the *opposite* of what

they expect. It's a part of the fine art of bullshitting and one that more Black folks need to adopt. It's the ultimate way to frustrate the powers that be, and it might just save you from a trip to jail or a beat down.

In times of confrontation, doing the opposite is a great bullshitting tactic. It's fun to disarm people, and it's an incredible strategy to have at your disposal. I've been doing this stuff since I was young. In high school, during the summers I used to work at a factory in San Joaquin Valley canning peaches. It was a tedious job. I was working nights and I used to get a little cranky when I was tired. The supervisor picked up on my crankiness and started giving me the crappiest jobs in the factory. I guess he figured I had an attitude problem. Everybody dreaded the assignments that I got nightly—they were that bad. This supervisor thought that if he kept giving me the shit-work, I'd eventually just get pissed off and quit.

But that's not the way I work. It never has been. Instead, I put a bullshit plan together: to pretend that I loved doing these tedious tasks. I pretended that I loved them so much, that I began to ask for more of them to do. My supervisor's boss noticed how productive I was at those crappy jobs. He didn't see my efforts as me running my "Mr. Opposite" routine. Instead, he saw "one of the good ones" and rewarded my productivity and willingness to work at the jobs no one else wanted to do with a raise and a cushy desk job. My new job was so sweet that I could actually go out to my car and sleep for a couple of hours a night without being missed!

"Come on, Russ," you're saying. "That doesn't happen in the real world!"

Yes, it does. I know because it really did happen to me. The moral of this story was that I killed the dude with kindness and an ambitious attitude. He might not have liked me, but his supervisor did and I was rewarded for it. That was a calculated risk, after all, I could have just ended up getting loaded down with more extra crappy jobs. But as I've I said, the game is full of calculated risks. Sometimes, you get the calculations right. Sometimes, not so much. Letting people think they've won has worked out for me nine times out of ten.

As with most bullshit, this rule requires you to keep your emotions in check. Or to think of it another way, you have to think of yourself as playing chess while others play checkers. Checkers is playing small, letting your emotions dictate your progress. If you let your emotions get in the way—if you end up cussing people out or whipping their ass, instead of finding a way to respond with your brain—you'll lose in the end. In the workplace, you'll burn a bridge that one day you'll discover you still needed. In your daily life, you'll find yourself in fist fights in the checkout line. With cops, you'll find yourself on the receiving in of a beat down.

Play it smart. Do the opposite, and when you're faced with a tough situation, a challenge or some of life's ugliness, let the other person think they're winning and stand aside to let Karma kick their ass.

RULE #10:

Talking Loud and Changing Nothing

(The Amplification of Bullshit)

They go by lots of names, but every workplace has one. Instigator. Unofficial employee advocate. Self-appointed "grievance committee." I call him or her the work place "lawyer"—though usually this person has never been to law school and his or her job title is more likely to be something like "Assistant"—just "Ass" for short. Whatever the educational background or specific title, it won't take you long to find out who this person is. Usually he or she will come to seek you out if you're new on the job. After all, he needs you. He needs everyone. He has to get you on his "side."

This self-appointed grievance committee has to have *everyone* on his side, usually against management, but occasionally against another employee. This workplace advocate will be the first one in your face to tell you that you're being treated badly. He'll be the first one to suggest that you file a complaint. He'll be the first one to propose that you come to a "meeting" with some others from the office who are determined to "do something" about what's going on.

Stay away from these people. Avoid them like the plague. Being aligned with the "grievance committee"—or whatever other name you'd like to give these angry folks—is a sure way to keep you from SWB.

"FUCK YOU!"

Early in my career, when I was working with KLOS in Los Angeles, things were going pretty well for me. Sure, there were things that weren't perfect, but on the whole, I was a good little talent and felt that management recognized and rewarded my efforts. Things didn't seem to be going as smoothly for one of my co-workers, Frazer Smith. You remember him. We worked together later on the video/variety show *Rock 'N' America.*

Frazer had lots of complaints about KLOS and was always going off on the bosses. He was, and still is, a talented comedian, but sometimes his ego got the better of him. I think some might have gone so far as to call him a "temperamental ego-maniac," but you didn't hear that from me. He had a reputation for screaming, yelling and causing trouble.

"Fuck you!" he'd scream at the boss after one of his many, many meetings about what was wrong at the station and how he was being screwed over. "Russ, are you with me?"

"No," I'd say with a big grin on my face. "Absolutely not."

Thanks to that grin, he couldn't tell if I was joking or not, but even though I smiled when I said it, I was serious as I know how to be. I wasn't down with his program in the least. Not at all.

It wasn't like I didn't like him. I did. He was (and still is) a cool guy. He's fun to be around, talented as hell and never did or said anything to hurt me inside the workplace or out of it. But neither had management. In fact, most of the bosses at KLOS were doing everything they could to help me develop my talent and explore all the opportunities available to me. Much as I liked Frazer, I had no reason to get involved with his issues with the station. As much as I appreciated the management's treatment of me, I couldn't say absolutely that Frazer didn't have some legitimate grievances with them, either.

So, my strategy was simply to stay out of it altogether. When asked about what was going on, I simply said, "I'm not in that" or "I mind my business," or I cracked a joke that made me as neutral as Switzerland in World War II. If you didn't know that Switzerland was neutral in World War II, once I again, I refer you to Google™. Or a history textbook. Your education is seriously lacking and you might want to address that before you make any further employment moves—or attempt any jokes in which you declare yourself not a party to any intra-office controversies.

Don't forget: all offices are cliques. The entertainment

industry can be particularly incestuous, but it doesn't matter where you work. Whether you work in a restaurant or health care or the prison industrial complex, the point is you do not want to be aligned with any group when an issue divides the workplace into camps. You want to be friendly with all sides, but a member of none. Trust me, no matter how oblivious the boss or management or supervisors may appear to be, they know *exactly* who is aligned with whom. They know which people are members of which camps. They know who is in the angry mob, and who isn't. And guess what? Members of the angry mob get picked off one by one. *Leaders* of the angry mob may remain (they might have just enough legitimate complaints to keep them from getting fired), but they don't move up the ladder. They don't do much cash-checking, and I know that's true because of what happened to my friend, Frazer.

Frazer lost his job with the radio station. I'm sure it was because of all the "fuck yous" and the screaming and shouting. Being talented is wonderful, but it won't protect you when the boss perceives you as a trouble maker. Frazer does stand-up now, and if he tours your city you should definitely check him out because he's a funny guy, but radio money is much better than stand-up money and heck of a lot more regular. It's a lesson in cash-checking. An occasional complaint, especially if it's legitimate, justified and presented in a manner that doesn't include a shouted "fuck you," won't hurt the number of digits on your paycheck—and might even add a few over the long term. A regular habit of complaints and repeated use of profanity will lead you straight to the unemployment line, without exception.

If one of your co-workers is in a dispute, either with the boss or with another co-worker, the smartest thing for you to do is refuse to get involved. Choose your battles carefully. I have worked with people that want you to fight their battles for them. When you don't, they label you as weak, selfish, out for yourself or a management suck up. Fine, but the reality is that *they* are probably all the things that they have accused you of being. If they weren't, they'd fight their own battles, wouldn't they? So when they ask you to tarnish yourself for them, don't do it. Just say "no."

Back in the day when I had my little record label, Rapsur Records, I was one of the few acts that got paid by the distributor, Macola Records. Don McMillan owned

Macola Records and his company distributed all of us who were LA rappers during the mid-eighties: JJ Fad, *LA Dreamteam, Bobby Jimmy and the Critters,* the list goes on and on.

Hardly anyone was getting paid in a timely manner, and we were pretty sure that was because Macula was selling our records off the books, thus lowering the amounts due to us. I can remember sitting in the lobby of Macola Records, waiting to see Don and hearing the sounds of a shotgun being cocked because Don hasn't paid some 'hood cat and the dude was coming for him.

Alonzo from the *World Class Wreckin Cru* called a meeting. "What we gotta do," he said to the group of us, "Is all go in together and get our money!" There were cheers of support from most of the guys, but I didn't say a word.

That's because I was getting my checks from Don on the regular and not because of any shotgun. Instead, I was getting paid because I was on defcon 4 level bullshitting of this man. "Your wife is so beautiful," I'd say. "You're really running a great business, here," I'd say. Hell, I said whatever he wanted to hear, then I'd take my check and leave!

There was no reason for me to join Alonzo's angry mob. Why should I? I don't know if they actually did storm the offices, but I do know I continued to get paid and they didn't. It's hard to not pay someone you like, and I made sure Don liked me. My fellow rappers needed to read this book. They hadn't learned to play the game behind the game. They didn't know that it's okay to kiss the ass of the hand that feeds you! It works much better than shotguns and angry words!

"WE GOT YOU, MAN"

Workplace advocates seem like they've got your back. They'll be the first ones to point out that there may be a problem and that you might be being overlooked or mistreated. Remember in Rule Number Ten, when I gave you some valuable advice about what to do when someone steals your ideas? This is a pop quiz. What do you say?

Very good class. You let the boss take the credit. You even let your co-worker take credit. You keep your head down, nose clean and your attitude positive because cream rises, and while it's easy to take credit, it's hard to deliver when you don't really have any ideas of your own. Karma will get idea-theives. You don't have to do anything.

The workplace advocate will be the first person who gets in your face after your idea gets hijacked.

"That was just wrong, man. Just wrong!" He'll say, trying to stoke both your ego and your sense of the unfairness of the situation. "Everyone in the room heard you say that first. But that's the way things go around here. The people who do the real work around here are always gettin' screwed. I think you should demand a meeting. And we—me and this one and that one—we got your back."

If you should end up having a conversation like this with someone in the office, someone who sounds as though they're sincerely concerned and sincerely interested in helping you right an office wrong—whether it's over a stolen idea, a missed promotion, or anything else—take my strong advice.

Run like hell.

Just say, "It's cool" and keep moving. Don't let yourself get talked into doing something that will mess up your game behind the game and forever align you with the angry crowd. Think of me and Macola Records. Think of cash-checking. Think of Karma—just don't get talked into anything you'll certainly regret!

SNITCHING

The other thing you don't want to do when there are disputes and controversies going on in the office is snitch. By snitch I mean tell the boss, or inform one party what the other party is saying. Say nothing.

I know snitching works for some people. They know who they are. You know who they are. Everybody knows who they are, but no one ever tells. It might be common knowledge in the office that "so-and-so is sleeping with so-and-so," but when the wife gets the anonymous email, everyone knows who did it. Everyone knows who the office snitch is, even if no one ever says it.

When I say "everyone," I really do mean everyone, including the boss. The snitch has a reputation, and once you get a reputation, it will follow you throughout your career. The business world is small, much smaller than you think. If you plan to keep working in the same industry or field, the chances are good that you're going to run into the same people again. The person you snitch on today might be your boss tomorrow. He's never going to forget you—you can count on it.

When it comes to workplace snitching, once again, I believe in Karma. No matter how slick you do it, it's gonna come out as tattling, and whatever you think you might be gaining, you're going to lose the boss' respect in the end. There's only one exception to my "no snitching" rule, and that is that if your work is directly affected by what the other person is doing, then you have a responsibility to say something.

"I don't want to get anyone in trouble, but this affects my ability to do my job . . ." That's how I'd start it. You might be able to think of some other helpful way of bringing up the topic, but you definitely want to try to be as tactful as possible. You want to state it in a way that makes it clear that you are reluctant to do what you're doing, and you're only doing it because it's in the best interest of the entire workplace. In that case, your reputation will certain suffer with the person who you're turning in, but it probably won't suffer with the people who sign your paychecks.

Speaking of reputations, snitching isn't the only reputation you'll never live down. If you're someone who gets a reputation for going to HR for the even the slightest perceived unfairness, if you've gotten yourself a reputation for whining and complaining anytime there's extra work that needs to be done, if you've earned a reputation for calling in sick almost every Friday—man, people know. You've lost all credibility. After a while, no one will take you seriously, even if you really have a problem, complaint or personal issue. You're a wrap. You're done. Unless you're able to do something that completely changes your reputation, you'll never be seen as anything other than the snitch, the complainer, the whiner, or the slacker, and changing your reputation isn't as easy as you might think. Unless you're moving on to a new job far, far away, creating a new rep can take years and years, if it ever happens at all.

It's much smarter not to develop a negative reputation in the first place. Instead, work on developing a reputation for being hardworking, positive and neutral as Switzerland.

RULE #11:

Know Your Enemies

(But Don't Let Them Know You Know They're Assholes)

If you've got a job, you've got enemies, or at least people who don't wish good things for you. I'm not talking about the people who make their hostility known. I'm not talking about the people who will get right up in your face and say, "I don't like you." In the workplace, smart people never do that, though if you work with dumb motherfuckers, it's possible that they might do it. That's another reason why Rule Number Seven is important. Dumb motherfuckers always end up doing something stupid and you don't want their stain anywhere near you.

The good thing about dumb motherfuckers is that they are easy to defeat, so we're not really worried about them. In the smart work environment, your real enemies are on the down low. If you're paying attention, you can tell who they are even when they're smiling in your face.

I always know who doesn't like me, who's uncomfortable with me, who's threatened by me and who might not have my best interests at heart. It's partly a "gut" thing—a feeling that you get based on subtleties that we talked about in Rule Number Eight. The "gut" feeling is typically accompanied by all kinds of body language that, if you know how to read it, will tell you everything you need to know about who's in your corner and who's not.

IDENTIFYING THE ENEMY

One of my father's favorite sayings was, "Know your enemy." When the enemy is undercover, you have to know how to read the signs. When people are uncomfortable with you, they let you know in all kinds of little ways that a master of the game behind the game can easily recognize.

They won't look you in the eye for example—or not for very long. If their eyes are darting all around while you're talking to them, something's up.

They may not want to touch you. If the handshake is particularly limp or non-existent, something's up. Similarly, if the handshake is over the top firm that's an "I'm trying to intimidate you" shake, and something's up.

They don't say much. If they don't want to talk to you, or don't seem to volunteer little about themselves in conversation, but always seem to be paying close attention when you talk about yourself, something is up.

If they stop talking when you walk up on them while they are in a conversation, something is definitely up.

If they have something critical to say about everything that comes out of your mouth, something is up.

If they seem to be talking down to you, or talking to you like you're stupid something's up. If there's always a high degree of sarcasm or attitude in their tone, even if they swear they're "joking," something is definitely up.

You may think the person who's acting strangely toward you is just "weird" and probably acts the same way toward everyone. I wouldn't assume that. It may be true, but even if it is, that doesn't necessarily change your response.

What is your response to a person who has either declared themselves your rival in the workplace or seems to be sending out a signal that they are extremely uncomfortable in your presence? What's your response to someone seems dubious about you?

You launch a charm offensive. You hark back to Rule Number One, Rule Number Three and Rule Number Ten. You bring on the bullshit. You launch a charm offensive and you *make* them love you.

"Russ," you're saying. "Suppose I know for a certain fact that this MF—excuse me, I mean *individual*—hates my guts?

So what? You're a bullshitter. You're an opposite man or woman—or you should be, if you've been reading this book carefully. You're playing the game behind the game now, and that means you're a strategic thinker. I have worked with people that have literally dogged me out behind my back and I knew it. I knew every negative thing they had to say about me. Most people would want to jam them up, and to make them pay for what they said. Nooooooo. Don't do that.

People who dog you are doing you a favor. They are making their feelings known. Now, you know who they are. Don't say anything. If you say anything, if you react emotionally, they win. If you let them know you're bothered, you hand them a victory. Don't let them win by going back at them hard. Instead, think about it strategically.

Here's how a strategic thinker analyzes the situation. Typically, when someone doesn't like you, they expect you to return the favor. They expect you will act like you two are mutual "enemies." You won't speak to them, either. You will avoid their company, too. You, too, will speak in sarcasms or veiled insults.

A bullshitter doesn't play that game. A bullshitter plays by different rules altogether. A bullshitter plays the opposite.

Instead of meeting dislike with dislike, kill them with kindness. Use their discomfort to your advantage. Frustrate them by refusing to give them the response they expect. Anytime you're able to frustrate someone's expectations, especially an enemy, *you* win.

I had a boss back in LA who had an unfortunate tell. You know what a "tell" is, right? You play a little poker? You know that a "tell" is an unconscious habit that someone has that lets everyone know what kind of cards they are holding. In the workplace, a "tell" doesn't signal two pair. It signals what someone is thinking or feeling about a person or a situation.

Back to my boss with the unfortunate tell. His cheeks would get red when he was starting to feel uncomfortable or upset. Really unfortunate, because everyone knew when he was annoyed, angry or in the presence of someone he didn't like by the deepening color on his face. Once I figured it out, I knew I had him. I'd see the color coming and then go out of my way to be extra, extra nice. I never let him know that I knew he was mad and that he was getting madder by the calm way I was talking to him.

It was fun to fuck with that guy. The best part is you can't get in trouble for being nice, calm and rational. It's the best way to really get on someone's nerves. It often works particularly well for me because I'm a fairly large Black male. With my exterior comes all types of stereotypes, usually associated with violence and confrontation, especially from some (though certainly not all) White people. Giving them the opposite of what they expect from me works to my advantage. With a smile and some bullshit, all of their preconceptions disappear. Now they don't know what to expect. They are confused. It works. Now, I don't automatically assume that all White people hold me in contempt because of my skin color, and you shouldn't either. You should know that using this piece of strategic bullshit to disarm someone who hasn't prejudged you based on race doesn't work very well. For those circumstances, you'll need different strategies, but on the occasion where race sets up unfairly negative expectations, bringing on the bullshit is an excellent strategy!

I use humor all of the time to disarm people who aren't sure what they think of me. For example, when I shoot movies with really famous, big time actors I use this strategy. I'm talking about people who earn $5,000 a day—a *day*—just to show up on the set. My attitude on those folks is to get their scenes done quickly and get them out of there. They're driving up my costs. Sometimes, these are people who, while they've taken the job, aren't sure about me. They aren't sure I know what I'm doing. They aren't sure I'm in their league. Sometimes, these are also actors who have a very ego-centric work ethic. They want to take up time. They want to use up *your* time. They want to go over things and over things. They can be demanding. They can be annoying.

So, when they start working *their* game on me, I say things like, "If you do that again, I'm going to kick your ass" in a very, serious voice, with a smile on my face.

You can tell by the looks on their faces that they don't know if I'm kidding or not.

"You're joking right, Russ?" they'll say, smiling uncertainly. "You're kidding."

"Sure, sure," I'll say, laughing a little. Then, just as fast as I started laughing, I'll go serious. "But I can kick your ass, and I will, if you do that again." Then I smile. Of course I would never resort to violence. (Unless we're running way over budget).

Huh? What?

"Russ, I can't tell when you're serious and when you're joking?"

"Really?" I say, and then I'm back to whatever the business at hand was. I leave them trying to figure me out. I know they don't like that they can't read me, but that's a win for me. I've been pleasant, I've stayed calm. No one's cussing anyone out and no one is saying anything nasty. No one's yelling or screaming. Everything is cordial and pleasant. And because everything is pleasant, calm and completely without animosity, what else can you do but hedge your bets? What else can you do but smile, be pleasant and cordial, and do your job?

They stop whatever crap they were pulling—just in case I meant that I was going to kick ass—and do a phenomenal job in one day. Sometimes on one take.

I love confusing people.

In your workplace, the same game behind the game works. The nicer you are, the more gentle you are, the more you keep your voice down and speak with a smile—especially to people who dislike or distrust you—the harder it is for them to run *their* game on you. In fact, it's just about impossible. They get angrier or more frustrated or just plain old confused, and you win every time.

RULE #12:

Handling Office Affairs Can be a Real Circus

When I say "work affairs," I don't mean the affairs of the office. I mean affairs, sexual ones, between people who work together. I have only one thing to say about those kinds of "hook ups":

Don't even think about it.

There's an old saying: "Don't shit where you eat." It applies perfectly to trying to combine a sexual relationship and your work environment. Sex in the workplace is a no-no and a no-go. People always think they can get away with it, and that it can help them move up the ladder, but 99 times out a hundred, sex in the office backfires. Sleeping your way up the corporate ladder ultimately undermines any respect you might have with everyone in your workplace. It also provides your enemies with powerful ammunition to use against you. These things are never "secrets"—someone always knows, or at least suspects. Just the rumor is enough to damage your prospects for advancement.

Sometimes, even flirting can be enough to create major trouble at work. Think about all of the laws that prohibit sexual harassment and inappropriate conduct. If you're not sure how something you say or do might be perceived in your office environment, don't say it and don't do it. I'm not just talking about members of the opposite sex. Even in same sex conversations, you can't assume that you can make comments that have sexual connotations. You don't know who is what or how they're going to hear what you're saying. That means lay off the gay jokes, skip the comments about other people's body parts (even if you mean them as compliments), and keep your descriptions of your personal status to a minimum.

With the new rules and laws, you can lose your job for just saying the wrong thing, even by accident. There are people laying in the cut, trying to get you, and if you don't know where the line is, you could end up finding out the hard way. Trust me on this one. I know what I'm talking about from experience. I've been caught with my pants down on this one, almost literally.

When I first joined WKYS in Washington, DC, I was playing the part around the office for a while as the wild and crazy new DJ from Texas. I was joking around with a co-worker and I made some comment about dropping my pants. I may have even reached for my belt buckle and started to undo it. Everyone was laughing and it seemed like everyone involved understood I was playing around.

I got called in to the boss' office.

"We heard you pulled your pants down in the hallway. Is this true?"

I was stunned. I recounted my version of what happened—and no, my pants didn't come down at all, no skin was shown and my fly remained zipped. I was joking, I pretended to unbuckle my belt, and that was the end of the story. My boss gave me a serious talking to about what was and wasn't appropriate in the work environment, even for a wild and crazy radio DJ from Texas. I didn't enjoy it, but I consider myself lucky. I could have gotten fired right then and there.

In time, however, I discovered *who* got me called into the boss' office like that. There was a lady in the office who had decided that I was going to be her next conquest. She'd been steadily making advances toward me, and I'd been steadily rejecting them. I guess she was on the "get back," because she's the one who ran to the boss and added her own bullshit to the story. It was more than a little embellishment to say that I'd dropped my pants in the hallway, and unfortunately for her, she hadn't read this book. She wasn't skilled enough to know that too much bullshit is a bad thing. She wasn't smart enough to realize that, while a little bullshit can be useful, too much bullshit comes down to just an outright lie. Her plot didn't work, but I was reminded of two important lessons—watch your back and don't even joke about anything below the waist in the work place. Don't joke about anything above the waist either. I can't quite say "don't joke at all," but be very careful, especially with anything that has to do with sex or sex organs or even body parts. As I said at the introduction of this section, be very sure of your audience. Think before you open your mouth, and if you're not sure, keep your damn mouth shut!

Once you get a reputation for screwing someone on the job, you'll never have credibility for succeeding on your own ability. When that relationship ends, and it will, you will be sitting in HR trying to explain yourself. Trust me on this: it will happen. There's no free ride, and playing with sex on the job is literally playing with fire. Every now and then someone gets away with it, but most people don't. Assume you're more likely to be the one to get caught and fired than the one who gets promoted and you'll be in good shape.

One other thing, before we leave this topic. If you do have an on the job affair, and you get fired, *don't* mention that you were fired for screwing around on the job in your next job interviews! This is the ultimate DNS (Dumb Negro Syndrome) topic. When asked why you left your prior employment, use your ability to bullshit to tap dance out an excuse, but the last thing you want to do when you're trying to get a new job is advertise that you got put out of the old job for being a whore. It's not a selling point. But who would do that? No one's *that* stupid, right? You'd be surprised.

RULE #13:

Mastering the Art of Bullshit and Its Shitfalls

(Okay, It Should Be 'Pitfalls' But Me and the Publisher Thought it Was Creative)

Like most confident bullshitters, I'm good at what I do (if I don't tell myself that no one else will). I've followed the rules that I've been sharing with you in this book, and I reached a pretty fair level of success. I'm actually at the point in my career where some people begin to look up to me as an "expert," and that means I'm also at the point in my career where there are a few pitfalls that could sabotage my ability to stay at the top of my game. These pitfalls—or should I call them "shitfalls" since we're talking about more bullshitting here—apply to people at all levels of the game behind the game, but they're particularly important to those who aspire to the pinnacles of SWB. Whether shitfall or pitfall, being able to distinguish the difference "ego" and "expertise" can save you a lot of heartache, embarrassment and drama whatever your work environment.

Most people think they know what "ego" means, but once again, I think you should get out your dictionary and see if it means what you think it means. Don't worry. I'll wait. I looked it up again myself and I think it's a good thing to do every so often. So many times, people go around using words when they don't really know what they mean and it's good to be willing to educate yourself every so often. I'd define it for you, but I really don't think that's good for you. After all this is a "self-help" book. How are you going to help yourself if you're not willing to do a little work?

Okay. Got it? Good.

I want to tell you the story of my friend. Okay, I don't actually have a friend like this. I made him up for educational purposes, but I bet you have a friend like this. If you don't, I bet you know someone just like him—you can't tell him nothing. I mean that. You can't teach him anything, you can't tell him anything. You can't help him. Why?

He knows every damn thing. He's an expert on everything from coffee creamers to quantum physics. Bring up any subject, and this dude already knows all about it.

I know you know him, or someone just like him.

In the office, this kind of "expert" is his own worst enemy for several reasons. Because he thinks he already knows everything, he can't ask for the help he needs to learn new responsibilities. Because he thinks he already knows everything, he can't be mentored by anyone with more experience. Because he thinks he already knows everything, he can't be instructed. In fact, most people avoid him like an STD. While he might be a smart person who could, indeed, move up the corporate ladder, chances are pretty good that he'll be stuck in a fairly low-level position forever. No one is going to invest any time or energy in him because his "ego"—his need to believe in his own self definition that he's an expert—actually keeps him from becoming truly knowledgeable about anything.

Ego kills opportunity. It kills the opportunity to learn from others. It kills the willingness to learn something new. Ego comes in the workplace comes in many forms—our friend is just one of those forms.

You'll see ego and expertise in other ways. When the opportunity to learn something new or to implement a new method comes along, have you ever heard someone say, "Don't tell me how to do this job! I been doing this job for twenty years!"?

That's pure ego talking. That's ego talking like it is expertise. Sometimes the person really *does* know what they're doing, but real expertise knows that that there can always be another, better way to do something. True experts are always learning. True experts recognize that sometimes even people who *aren't* experts at all can offer a fresh perspective that can be useful, refreshing and valuable.

I think I told you some of my experiences early in my radio career, working with some of the really great broadcasters of their time at KABC radio and then at KDAY.

You could tell a lot about them by how they treated a new kid on the block like me. You could tell just how much of their game was "ego" and how much was "expert" by how willing they were to play with the new ideas I suggested. Some of the greatest guys in the business—guys like Bud Furillo who was truly one of the greatest sportscasters to ever work the microphone—were great about trying new things. Then there was the immensely talented Steve Woods, who while excellent at what he did, found it harder to relinquish his ego enough accept new ideas and embrace new talent. Seeing how these different personalities managed their egos and their expertise taught me the importance of developing one, and managing the other.

EGO

By the late 1980s KABC found it needed to "right size" or get rid of what they believed was an excess of employees. They offered a $50,000 buyout to anyone who was willing to take the money and go, thus trimming their staff.

I thought about it for all of two seconds, and then I took the money and ran. I was young and $50,000 in 1980s money was a lot of cash to check. I knew I would find another job somewhere and it just seemed like a smart gamble to make.

I ended up at KACE, another Los Angeles station, but only part-time, doing comedy bits for the overnight guy. They were supposed to audition me for my own show, but it never happened. The program director just didn't see me with a show at KACE, but another program director by the name of Jack Patterson got a copy of my audition tape and hired me to do bits at 1580 KDAY for Steve Woods, a legendary announcer in lack radio. That gig was also part time.

Steve had big deep voice and was extremely well known in radio. Eventually Jack hired me to work with Steve on a full-time basis. To hire me, he had to fire one of his best friends, but he did it because he really believed that Steve and I could achieve great ratings together.

First, let me say that working with Steve Woods was the opportunity of a lifetime for me. The man wasn't a comedic genius, but our combined talents produced some really great concepts. It was the sort of break in my career that I believed was the stepping stone I needed to "achieve my dreams." In one way, the job delivered. I created "Bobby Jimmy" while working with Steve. I owe a lot to Bobby Jimmy; he was a character I became known for who sounded something like Eddie Murphy's "Buckwheat" from *Saturday Night Live*. Before I worked with Steve, I didn't know I could do impressions, but on his show, I did Ronald Reagan, who was President at the time, and a bunch of other famous voices.

On air, we were a great team, but off the air, Steve was introducing me to another difficult lesson. As brilliant as he was, he was also highly threatened by new talent. Instead of nurturing me, he was threatened by me, and because of that, he acted out in very strange and inappropriate ways. Of course, the drugs and alcohol that ultimately killed him probably had something to do with it, too. Whatever the reasons, off the air, Steve and I often had a contentious relationship.

For example, once the *Los Angeles Times* was coming to do a story on us. The key word in that sentence was *us*. I believed that we were a team. I didn't know the exact day the newspaper reporter was coming, but one day when I arrived to do our show, Steve shut my microphone off.

"What are you doing?" I demanded.

"Turning off your mic. You're not working today. You might as well go home."

I was furious. I cursed him out (breaking my own rule about cussing out your boss), and then I went home for the day, not knowing the reporter was scheduled to arrive. When the *LA Times* article came out, it was all about Steve Woods. There wasn't a single mention of Russ Parr. It was like I didn't exist.

Unfortunately, that wasn't an isolated incident. Steve would get mad at me for any reason or no reason at all and shut off my microphone, or we'd get into arguments about different bits for the show and whether to do them. We crossed swords over matters great and small. The only times we got along were when we were on the air and when we were out drinking. I know Steve loved me, but he was also jealous. He was tremendously talented, but tremendously troubled, too.

I learned a lot from the experience, though. Working with Steve Woods taught me that you didn't need a big, golden voice to succeed. I had a bunch of little voices and characters, and they worked, just like they did when I was just entertaining my family in the basement of our house. He taught me how *not* to be in this business. I learned that I don't have to be threatened by younger talent, I can be supportive and encouraging. I can be a mentor. I can be to them what Steve failed to be for me.

I can be their JJ Johnson.

JJ Johnson was one of the best mentors in radio that I ever had. He was an on-air personality at 1580 KDAY who had many years of experience and knew the rules of the radio game. We worked the morning show together after Steve Woods left, and JJ taught me everything he knew. He knew that what he was teaching me would someday make him expendable. He was basically training me right into *his* job, but he believed that I had something special and he wanted to have a role in nurturing it, so he gave me the best of his knowledge. His ego took the backseat. Eventually, he did train me to succeed him and he lost his spot working morning drive with me. I owe him a debt of gratitude. If you're lucky enough to run into a mentor like JJ Johnson in your career, don't forget to pay the lesson forward. When the time comes, don't be threatened. Remember what you were given and pass it along to the next fresh-faced kid. I know it's what I hope to do.

DEVELOPING EXPERTISE AND MANAGING EGO

It probably won't surprise you to learn that the film industry is famous for the struggles between ego and expertise.

I've known I wanted to make movies since I was in high school and I've been working toward actually making them since junior college. Choosing to major in Radio, Television and Film meant that I had the opportunity to get the foundations of film in school, and I did some acting early in my career. For me, acting was partly about learning a bit about what it's like to be in front of the camera (and partly about making some extra money, since commercials pay well), but it's never been comfortable for me. In case you've been living under a rock and were totally unaware of it, acting is a highly competitive business. I can remember going to auditions and there would be literally hundreds of other actors there competing for the same thirty second commercial. It's hard to find ways to stand out from the crowd and impress a casting director with that kind of competition. The sheer numbers of wannabes make acting hard work. I confess, for me, it was just *easier* to be in front of the microphone than in front of the camera. Pursuing radio came more naturally to me than pursuing a career as an actor.

Writing screenplays was something I just decided to start doing. I never thought I could write a script, but in 1996, I just sat down and wrote *The Last Stand.* The story was loosely based on my life as a stand-up comic and being a young father. I didn't realize I could write a script in less than a week. With a completed script in hand, I tried to shop the story around Hollywood, but there were no takers. I threw it in a drawer and there it stayed for 10 years.

One day I was cleaning out my desk and I found it again. Alfredas was visiting and I tossed her the script.

"Read this before I throw it away," I told her.

She called me back that afternoon.

"If you can't get anyone to do this story, you need to do it yourself."

So I did.

The Last Stand was the most autobiographical of my movies, but I pursue what interests me. To me, there are all kinds of interesting stories in the Black community that really haven't been explored in a thoughtful, nuanced way. There's lots of buddy-cop stories featuring Black actors. There are lots of sister-done-wrong dramas with Black actors and lots 'hood comedies featuring Black actors and comedians. I don't have anything against that—in fact, my film *Something Like A Business* is a parody of some those elements, but there are serious things we can write about, too. My film, *Thirty Five and Ticking*, is the story of four friends who are approaching that magic number. They're either single, unhappily married or they want a family and they're worried because the clock is running and they all want to find happiness before they hit the big 4-0. Then there's *Love for Sale*, a romantic comedy that I wrote and shot in fifteen days, which is about a lowly delivery guy who becomes a "boy toy" for a wealthy older lady. He needs the cash to try to win the girl he loves, but whole situation is complicated, in more ways than one. I've also written a couple of others I haven't produced yet—*The Shunning of Autumn*, which is a romance that explores the dark skin versus light skin colorism problem that has plagued the African American community since slavery—and unfortunately continues to do so. Then there's *The Under Shepherd*, a story about an televangelist who veers far off the spiritual path as he becomes absorbed by the money and power of his ministry. And *Dreams Stars are Made Of,* which is a Black thriller about an actress whose competitors are all disfigured one by one. You really don't know "who done it" until the last frame. *The Price of Love* is an adaptation of a book by Tanisha Bagley, chronicling her life as a victim of domestic violence. I also wrote a romantic dramedy called *Married But Single* that is about women married to professional athletes.

How's that for a 60 second advertisement for everything written, produced and about to be directed by Russ Parr? You hardly noticed it, right?

The point is, I'm disciplined about this, and I have long range plans to continue to make films as often as I can raise the money and find the time to shoot them. I love directing, and it comes as naturally to me as radio does. I think I'm getting good at it—certainly the movies have done okay, but making movies while Black is a lot like succeeding while Black.

It's tricky.

It's tricky because the market is scared of Black movies. When you're marketing a Black film, whether or not you get distribution might depend on whether Tyler

Perry's last film was a hit or not. If Tyler's last film didn't do so good, the powers that be are going to decide that "Black movies are out" and you're going to have trouble. Unfortunately, Black films are all put in the same box. We are judged as one, and not as individuals.

I wish I were joking, but I'm not. Dealing with how Hollywood sees Black movies is another book, another game within a game. For this book, let's stick to what you can learn about ego and expertise from my experiences in writing, directing and producing films.

Every industry and every work environment has its share of egos, but the entertainment industry is notorious for them, with film probably being among the worst. Because I value expertise, but I hate ego, I have some rules on my movie sets that are designed to keep expertise high and ego low. They are simply these:

1. No egos allowed;
2. Everyone's ideas count;
3. No yelling.

NO EGOS ALLOWED

This is easy to say, but you've got to crack the whip and make it clear that you mean it. I'm not just talking about actors. Everyone involved with a film, or any project for that matter, has their area of expertise, and people can get very touchy when they feel that their talents are being infringed on or aren't being appreciated. That's why I think it's important in any work environment for everyone to have a role, and to understand what that role is. I expect that there will be some overlap from time to time, and even some over-stepping. I expect that some people assert their egos to challenge me and others as a way of making sure that we know what we're doing. There's a place for that in any workplace, and it's a way of testing the boundaries, and asking for reassurance. It's like little kids, testing the waters to see how far they can go before they get smacked.

Can I go this far?

This far?

Pow!

Guess that's the limit!

It's important to know your role and stay (mostly) in your lane. But I also like to encourage everyone to bring their ideas about the entire project to the table. A successful endeavor needs to be flexible enough to allow everyone the chance to contribute. That leads me to my second rule.

EVERYONE'S IDEAS COUNT

Great people are the key to a great product, and the truth is that everyone has a spark of creativity inside them. Regardless of what their job title on the film is, I think it's important to acknowledge everyone's creativity. I know that pisses some people off, but I don't care. When I do a film, everyone, regardless of their job title, can participate.

Here's a story that proves that point.

When we were shooting the film *35 and Ticking*, there's a scene where one of the characters leaves his wife. The way it was originally written, the husband, played by Dondre Whitfield, comes home and finds his bags packed for him. He was supposed to grab his bags and leave. It was supposed to be very dramatic and we had already done one take when one of the young ladies working on the production tapped me on the shoulder.

"Excuse me," she said. "I hope I'm not out of place here, but I had an idea and I wanted to share it with you."

Now the AD, the Assistant Director, was standing near me, and it was clear that he wanted to move on to the next scene. You have to remember that shooting a feature film in 15 days is rough, and you really don't have a lot of spare time. I'm sure he didn't even want to hear what the lady had to say, but my rule is that everyone can participate, so I let her know that I was ready to listen to whatever she wanted to say.

"I just thought, since he's leaving her, maybe he could take off his ring and just leave it there. Leave it on the bed."

I knew as soon as she said it that it was what the scene was missing. I thanked her and we shot it. It's in the film right now. When you see it, remember this story—that scene wasn't my idea or one of the ideas of one of the so-called "creative" people. It was the idea of the lady who had just recently joined the production. I don't remember what her function was, and it doesn't matter. Her idea was a good one and we used it.

Everyone has a creative thought. Everyone. If you alienate people by sending off that signal that you think that you are above them, in the end you will be the one who suffers for that attitude. Your superior attitude will cost you opportunities, both in contacts and in cash-checking. That lady's idea about the ring was a perfect example. If I had blown her off, or sent out such a strong vibe of ego that she never even bothered to approach me, we would have lost that scene. We never would have gotten that image, and the movie would have been worse off for it.

It's important to be spontaneous. It's important not to be so threatened by what's "new" or "different" that you can't embrace it. It's important not to be so afraid that people will find out that you "don't know" that you can't receive the new information you need. This is true in every industry. Certainly it's true in the entertainment business, which often changes very quickly. It really doesn't matter what your business is, or what business you want to be in. You have to be open to new information. You have to be willing to receive the creative impulses that come from others. You have to be willing to shut up and listen.

NO YELLING

My last rule is that there's absolutely no yelling at anybody allowed on my movie sets. No yelling in anger, no berating of anyone and absolutely no grandstanding, trying to call attention to oneself or playing the diva. We're here to work together to produce something that the viewers will enjoy. There's no reason for anyone to bring an ego to the set or the show, and as a result, there's no reason to bring the by-products of ego—yelling and screaming and causing scenes—to the show. No one wants to pay an asshole, including me. I want to pay one of the good ones.

I practice what I preach about yelling. I truly believe yelling is counter-productive.

In my entire career, I think I've yelled at three people —all Black people, and all people that I really cared about and wanted to see succeed. I yelled because I wanted them to know that what I was doing was nothing compared to what other people in this life might subject them to. My yelling was a private affair, and I didn't yell at them in front of other people.

Now hear me out. While I don't believe in yelling, I do think there's a place for anger in the work place. Anger can be very productive when it's done professionally. You have to be armed with facts, though. Spouting off emotionally is foolish and will only hurt you, but anger, delivered coolly and calmly and accompanied by a long list of facts, is better than fireworks to light up a bad situation. Calm, cool, professional anger is absolute dynamite that can lead to serious cash-checking because all of the sudden, management is like, "Uh, oh. This guy is serious, and he has his shit together. We better listen to him and maybe we should kick him upstairs, too!" Think about it. Even if you're working at Mickie D's, if you get calm, cool and professionally angry because people are screwing up the fries, management's going to take notice. You're angry, but you're angry because you care about the customers.

I smell fries . . . and a promotion. I smell cash-checking.

Personal anger in the work environment is never productive. Never. You won't win, even if you are right. People get fired over personal differences with their boss, and they can get disciplined for personal differences with other members of the staff. Don't get personal at work, and don't let personal issues interfere with work responsibilities. That's a lose-lose situation, and no one who aspires to be a master bullshitter would allow themselves to get sucked into that. In a way, falling into personal dramas at work is a way of expressing one's ego in another way. It's a way of making the workplace "all about me" instead of all about the job.

No matter how it's expressed, ego stunts your professional growth. Ego kills. I don't want to be one of those guys who spouting off about "I been in this business for twenty years." I'd like to think I've reached a level of expertise, but I'd also like to think that I'm able to learn from younger people and from people whose experiences are different from my own. I like to associate with younger people and with people who know things I don't know. I hope that I'm the sort person who is secure enough in his knowledge not be threatened by what others might try to teach me. I hope that I'm flexible enough to re-invent myself daily.

What you want to learn from these stories I'm telling you is that you want to develop your knowledge in every way that you can, without letting your ego take over the picture. Ego, in any industry, is a big shitfall. Step over it. You never want to become that person who can't learn, and you never want to be the person who lets ego block them from receiving what other people have to offer.

RULE #14:

Put the Power of Negative Thinking to Work for You in a Positive Way

This book has been about how to the play the game behind the game. It's been about how to succeed while Black. It's about the business of "cash-checking." Since it is about success, you might think that in this last chapter, I'm going to encourage you to "reach for your dreams." You might think that I'm going to try to inspire you to "achieve your goals." You might think that I'm going to tell you to "think big."

Wrong. All that "achieve your goals" stuff is just some bullshit, and I should know. I have a doctorate in bullshit. Thinking big is so over-rated. I've met a lot of big thinkers and I'll tell you where a lot of them end up—suffering with DNS (Dumb Negro Syndrome). Thinking big often leads people into trying to do bigger shit than they have the skills for. The result is disaster. For example, why does every NBA star start a record label, only to see it go under after they've spent about $40 million? Why do rap stars give themselves a nickname that usually gets them busted? (Note to the aspiring hip hop artist: nicknames like Kilo, Murder, OG, Chronic, Meth etc., won't give you "street cred," they'll just get you booked at County. If you don't have the skill set to take your brand to the next level, skip the nicknames and focus your energy on finding someone who does!)

You see my point? Having goals is great. Working on achieving goals is great, but expecting to achieve them, especially on a certain timeline or in a certain way, isn't part of how I play the game. Instead, you're better off embracing the power of negative thinking.

Yeah, you heard me. *Negative* thinking.

POSITIVELY CRAZY

There's a lot of talk about positive thinking. Everybody saw that movie, *The Secret*, a few years back, and suddenly being successful has a whole new vocabulary. "Speak as if it were already so," some of you are saying to each other. "Live as if it were already so!"

You people are watching too much *Oprah*. Thinking positively is nice, but in the real world, it has nothing to do with getting anywhere. Having a goal is nice, but a goal alone is useless if you don't know how to play the game. Living your life with a purpose is good, too, but unless you're able to anticipate and manipulate the *other* people who are operating in your life, you'll never get as far as you would if you stopped focusing on *thinking* and started *doing*.

A negative thinker has a goal and a plan. A negative thinker works hard toward achieving that goal or plan, but unlike the positive thinkers who invest a lot of emotional energy in "believing," a negative thinker keeps his or her energy on his actions and the emotional expectation low. A negative thinker shoots for the stars, but knows that in reality, actually reaching the stars is just about impossible. A negative thinker is more than willing to be pleasantly surprised by life if things work out, but has a back-up plan for when they don't, just in case.

I don't mean to burst anyone's bubble here. I don't mean to bring the rain after you just had your perm touched up. I don't mean to kill all the unicorns, but this is the *reality*. Reality means that things usually don't work out as planned. Personally, I'd rather have a big goal, and work my ass off—knowing that the getting there might never happen—than be completely destroyed every time things don't come together like I planned.

I've known too many people who were ready to slit their wrists because they didn't reach a goal by some completely bullshit timeline of their own making.

"Oh no! I didn't make my first million dollars before thirty!"

"If I didn't throw my back out during a tip drill, I would be getting rained on more than any girl in this club!"

"Damn it, I'm seventeen and I haven't earned a Grammy yet. What is the point of living?"

It's ridiculous.

Sure, have goals. Have dreams, too. In fact, most of the biggest successes I've had in life came from dreams. Actual dreams. The kind you have at night. Maybe that's weird, but it's true. I can remember imagining myself doing what I'm doing now when I was a teenager. I remember dreaming about myself making movies around the same time in my life. Maybe I'm psychic? Okay, probably not, but I can tell you for certain that I didn't sit back and say "I dreamed it. So now I'll just sit back and wait for the Universe to bring it to me." No. I took actions toward reaching those goals. It's been much more about the *work* than the thinking. If I'm thinking at all, I'm thinking about down-playing my hopes. I'm thinking about managing my expectations. The fact is that I've seen a lot of very, very talented people fail. I've seen a lot of deserving people passed over, including my own father when he was passed over in his quest for a higher rank. That was the first time I had ever seen my dad cry. I was devastated. The guy was (and is) brilliant, but it didn't matter to the Air Force. Instead, my father, the Black officer, had to endure seeing a bunch of dumb

White people (sorry, but in this case it was true) elevated above him. I've never forgotten that. Sometimes you can be the best candidate, or the most brilliant person in the room and never even get a chance. Seeing that teaches you to always keep yourself grounded. It teaches you to keep working and looking for ways to make your own chances, independent of the Universe or anything else.

Expecting the worse, believing in the power of negative thinking, will always leave you grateful when life hands you the best it has to offer. Playing up the negative can also be a powerful strategy in helping you to get information, gain allies and keep on cash-checking.

Some of my earliest experiences introduced me to just how quickly things can change and how much better it can sometimes be to expect things to fall apart. Maybe that's why I accentuate the negative. If things don't work out, I know I can just go into "fuck it" mode and wait for things to get better.

LOSS

As I've mentioned in earlier rules, when I was 16, my mother died. It was completely unexpected and our family was never the same.

My mom, Betty Ann Parr, was an amazing woman. She was very smart, very loving and a very hard worker. As a kid, I watched her create a completely new identity for herself—from housewife to school teacher. She balanced her family responsibilities and her schoolwork, and then later she balanced her roles as wife and mother with her job responsibilities. She was an intensely creative and innovative person and was very dedicated to the kids she taught. She was the kind of person who brought her work home, and I mean that literally, because as I've said she was always bringing home kids who were troubled or who needed help. Sometimes she was able to help them, and sometimes they took advantage of her kindness, but it never stopped her. She felt it was part of her responsibility to help people, to try to take care of them.

She was also very beautiful woman. In the late 60s and early 70s, I remember her wearing mini-skirts and keeping up with the looks that were in style. I remember listening to her talk to my sister about poise, about being a woman, and about what to expect from men. I learned a lot about how to treat a woman from eavesdropping on those conversations.

My mother saw that I had a lot of talent and she encouraged me to pursue my interests at an early age. I expected to have her encouragement for years and years into the future. It wasn't to be.

One day in my senior year of high school, I was summoned to the office. My mother had broken her ankle a few weeks before. She had a cast on her foot that was really giving her trouble. Her toes were blue and she kept going back to the doctor asking them to chip away at the cast, complaining that it was too tight.

"We can't take off too much more of it, Mrs. Parr," the doctor kept telling her. "It won't do what it's supposed to do if it's not tight."

Mom accepted that, but she kept complaining about how it hurt. She was struggling emotionally, too. Her sister had died a year earlier, and then her father passed away. Those losses had hit her hard. They had been very close.

I thought it was something with her ankle when I left school and hurried to the hospital. When I got there and peeked into the room and saw the doctors pumping on her chest, trying to re-start her heart, I was shaken. It turned out to be a blood clot that had formed in her leg and travelled to her heart. They couldn't save her.

Later, I understood that she must have known. I remembered the light in her face that morning when I left for school. I remembered what she'd said to me the night before, "You're going to be okay, Russ. You're going to be okay." I knew she was worried about my brother and my sister, both of whom were struggling with the responsibilities of young adulthood in different ways. "You're going to be the strong one," she said to me in that conversation. "You're going to be okay."

I wouldn't look at her in the casket. I wanted to remember her the way she was.

Losing someone you love unexpectedly like I did changes the way you think about everything. It changes what you think of yourself and it changes what you believe about how the world works. It changes your expectations and your certainties. It's just a devastating thing. It brought my family closer in a way, but it also separated us as each of us tried to deal with our grief. My brother was in the Marine Corps and he was having his own struggles. He ultimately got involved with drugs. That was how he dealt with our mom's passing. He was able to get himself out of that life ultimately, and I'm very glad. I've always looked up to him.

My sister got married to the man she'd been seeing. My mom had liked him, but had not really felt that he was right for my sister. In the end, my sister realized my mom was right, but it was what she needed to do at the time to try to fill the void.

I stayed with my dad. We'd get up early in the morning and play golf and he'd talk. He taught me the rules I'm teaching you in this book on so many of those cold morning outings. That's when I first heard them and started living them. That's part of his legacy to me, an understanding of the game behind the game. My mother's legacy to me is her compassion. Merge those two together and you get Russ Parr.

The point is just this—Don't fall in love with your plans and expectations. Life happens to them and they can be so easily derailed. The power of negative thinking is that you're always anticipating just what can go wrong, or just how bad things can get. When bad news and betrayals happen, you're way ahead of it.

COMEDY: LESSONS IN LOW EXPECTATIONS

Comedy isn't pretty. It truly isn't. Doing stand-up is an experience that, if you haven't learned the power of negative thinking, you'll get a crash course pretty quickly. It's hard to explain how something can be so wonderful (hearing people laugh at your jokes) and so terrible (getting booed for the exact same jokes) at the same time. My experiences in that world taught me some powerful lessons about negative thinking and managing expectations.

I met some pretty well-known comics while doing stand up. I had the opportunity to audition for a regular spot at The Comedy Store. Mitzi Shore (Paulie's mom and Sammy's wife, one of the owners of the place) used to personally audition all the young comedians hoping to appear at The Comedy Store. For my audition, the comedian, Paul Mooney, sat beside her.

I did my set and I thought it went pretty well. I found out later that the whole time I was performing, Paul was muttering in Mitzi's ear, "Yeah, he's good, but he ain't ready. He ain't ready." In hindsight, I probably *wasn't* ready, but I never forgot Paul Mooney. Remember what I taught you in Rule Number Three about not burning bridges? Years later, Paul's people wanted to book him on my radio show. You know what I did? I had him on. I don't believe he would have remembered me or the story of his part at my Comedy Store audition even if I had told him about it. I didn't tell him. I don't hold grudges. What's the point of that?

In comedy and in life, though, there are people who feel threatened by other people's talent. They feel like the pie is limited and if you get cut a slice of it, their piece just got smaller. Mooney was Richard Pryor's head writer at that time, so I don't believe his livelihood was threatened, but I know the competition between comedians is fierce and relentless. If you're funny and have some good material, expect it to get stolen, especially by more well-known comedians. Some of those guys would even send their "people" to the shows to write down the good jokes and bring them back. I'd go to a show a week later and hear another comedian doing my whole act, while the crowd laughed. Did I get even a word of credit? Not one. Complaining about it is useless. It's the way things are done.

Comedy taught me two things about the power of negative thinking that are relevant, no matter what business or industry you're in. First, the better you are, the more likely it is that you should expect that someone will try to throw some shade on you. The second is that positive thinking is useless when you're standing on the stage in front of a waiting audience with nothing at all to say because the guy who performed in front of you just ripped off your entire act. It's better to be cagey enough to always have a Plan B, whether it's an extra copy of a report, a witty comeback for a snarky co-worker or a few new jokes. I've had people take credit for my talent my whole my career, but I don't waste time defending myself. The game behind the game is bigger than one stolen credit. I'm bigger than one stolen credit.

I learned those lessons doing stand up, but I've found the power of negative thinking to come in handy in plenty of other situations. Learning to plan for the worst and even make it work for you, are good tools for anyone playing the game to have in their arsenal. Now let me throw you for a loop. My negative thinking is really positive thinking. Now I know y'all think I'm crazy, but it's about protecting yourself, and what could be more positive than that?

Negative thinking is the proof of that old adage, "All that glitters isn't gold." Negative thinkers know that when you step into an exciting new circumstance, it's wise to hold back. Nothing is as it seems and everything has its price. Everything. Paying that price is something negative thinking acknowledges, while positive fairy dust doesn't seem to recognize it at all.

Negative thinking makes you suspicious. I'm not saying you turn down opportunities, but when you accept, you accept with your eyes wide open. You accept, knowing that the game is in progress and that you've walked into it in full swing.

PLAYING THE UNDERDOG

It's human nature to root for people to fail, and if you think there aren't people rooting for you to fall on your ass right now, you are either in a drug-induced haze of happy talk or you haven't been paying attention to what I've spent the last hundred pages trying to tell you.

The better you're doing, the more likely it is that there are people, actively and vocally, expressing their hope to see you come toppling off your pedestal. This is why a negative thinker learns early to *shut up* about how great things are going. A negative thinker knows the haters are out there, and they'll come out of the woodwork sooner and do you more harm faster if you're running around talking about how you're "acting like it's so." Instead, a negative thinker learns to play the underdog.

When you speak to your co-workers, downplay your

talents. Don't talk about them at all if you can help it. Be excellent, work hard, give everything you do your very best, but don't say much about it. People will like you better.

I've been playing the underdog since I was teenager. The dynamics in my family were a little complicated when I was growing up. There was a lot of tension between my father and my older brother. They always seemed to be clashing over something. By comparison, I was the adored younger son whom my dad wanted to shape into what he wanted me to be.

The problem was, I adored my older brother. He was "King" to me. I didn't want to compete with him. I wanted to admire him, which I did. I wanted him to be happy. I wanted peace. My older brother had some athletic talent, but nothing particularly stellar, though he certainly enjoyed sports. By the time I reached high school, though, I had become a pretty good basketball player and was getting a lot of attention for how well I played that game.

It made me uncomfortable. I didn't want my brother to feel bad. I didn't want to seem like I was trying to compete with him for my father's attention or love, so I underplayed my athletic achievements. I didn't talk about them. If other people brought them up in my brother's presence, I changed the subject. Though I still played and gave my heart at every game, I went out of my way not to seem the least big arrogant about my skills. It's something I still do today, just not with basketball.

Today, when I play the underdog I'll say, "I only have 67 listeners." Sixty-seven listeners? That's pathetic! Poor guy, the audience thinks. He's pretty good. He should have more listeners than that. I'll tune it tomorrow. That sort of self-deprecating approach to my career keeps me acting and feeling like the underdog. People stay on my side. I've a gotten a few more listeners because of it, I think. I might be up to 70 by now.

I play the underdog with my bosses, too. Well, "underdog" might not be the right word. I play the *victim* with my bosses.

"Russ," they'll say. "We want to meet with you tomorrow after your broadcast for a few minutes, okay?"

"I'm getting fired, aren't I?" I'll say immediately. "Ratings are down and I'm out!"

"No, nothing like that."

"No, you're just saying that. I knew this day would

come. I knew it wouldn't last!" I work myself up a bit. I'm a guy with a PhD in bullshit, remember? I can't help it. "Okay, I'll have my desk cleaned out by noon." (Actually, I don't have a desk. I threw that in for visual effect. It's a little embellishment in action. See Rule Number One.)

"It's nothing like that! We just want to talk about . . .," and here I'll get an advance briefing on the content of the proposed meeting. Thank you very much. I now have the advance information that I needed to figure out my strategies and play the next round of *my* game (not yours!) at this meeting.

"Underdog" and "victim" are two of my favorite ways to get support. Now, for the record, I'm not actually a victim. I just play one to get further ahead in the game. Positive thinking strategies don't leave room for the usefulness of playing the victim. In fact, they reject victimhood, even deliberate and conscious victimhood, entirely. Too bad, I say. It's a good thing to be able to play a victim without ever incorporating "victimhood" as the truth of your identity. Negative thinking lets you experiment with all kinds of roles in order to find out which ones can help you to get to further cash-checking.

NEGATIVE TO POSITIVE

A last thought about negative thinking. Sometimes it's useful to bring up the negative to accentuate the positive. I set my goals high—so high that even I don't think it's possible I could actually get there. When my goal is outrageous, whatever I *do* get—especially if I get anywhere close to that outrageously unattainable initial goal—seems really, really good. If I don't get anywhere close, then I just say, "I wasn't supposed to get to that outrageous goal anyway" and I move on. It makes whatever result I actually *do* get for my efforts seem pretty darn good.

Sometimes, I do it the opposite way. I expect something so terrible that when it doesn't happen, whatever *does* happen seems good by comparison. It's like "I'm going to get fired, I'm sure of it." When you just get a pay cut, it's like, "Oh boy! At least I still have a job. Thank you, Jesus!" Maybe that's not the best example, but you get the idea. Negative thinking keeps my expectations low. I keep reaching for those stars and working toward those dreams, but there's always a part of me that will be okay if I don't get exactly what I expect. There's a part of me that's expecting to get taken down a peg, so I've always got a spare joke written on a napkin in my pocket.

CONCLUSION

If you're reached this page, then one of two things has happened. Either you have read all of my rules for succeeding while Black and are ready to launch yourself into my world—the world of cash-checking—or you have just decided to skip the middle and find out how it ends. You know which description fits you best. Here's the truth: your chances of success in the world have a lot to do with whether you are a "finisher" or a "skipper."

Here is my last rule, buried here in the conclusion for those who have seen this book through—Finish what you start. You can't expect to be successful, and you can't expect to be cash-checking if you take on projects and abandon them when they get difficult or when you get tired or when you don't like them or you get bored. This book was an easy test of your discipline because it wasn't hard to read (I used simple words and everything) and it couldn't possibly be boring, but if you skipped to the back, I think you have some questions to ask yourself about your level of commitment and discipline!

People who succeed in life don't succeed because they "got the hook up." They don't succeed by climbing over others, or even because they know how to bullshit. Ultimately, your success will come down to something inside you—a combination of determination, drive and discipline—that makes you work until it's done and keep going when everyone else has quit. That's true for everyone who is successful, regardless of their field, regardless of their race or their gender. You can't be a success and a quitter. It's just not possible.

I don't know where this trait comes from. I don't know if you're born with it, or if it's something that develops because of the circumstances that you face in your life. What I *do* know is that we all have at least some control over it. We all have faced the moment when we either say to ourselves "to hell with it" or "I'm not taking no for answer."

A bullshit artist knows how to charm others, that's

definitely true, but a master of the art of BS also knows how to talk to herself (or himself) and to convince herself to keep going for another day, even when she's tired, when things are difficult and even when she's bored. Sometimes, the most important person you need to able to bullshit is *yourself.* You need to be able to keep yourself believing. You need to have a dream in your mind that you'd like to see yourself achieve, so you can stand the long hard hours of mopping floors or dunking fries in hot oil. You need the image of yourself accepting awards if that's what turns you on, or riding in a limo, or simply of owning your own home and providing well for your children. You need to be able to keep that image in your mind even when it seems like you might never actually get there.

You have to be able to commit yourself to the process of advancing yourself, and sometimes that might take every trick in this book and a few more that you create on your own. You might have to work hard to convince yourself that doing what you're doing now is a step to something better. You have to think of a young Michael Jordan, putting in hours and hours, doing the basics of basketball, alone on the court. He didn't know he'd be the greatest to play the game while he was out there, night after night and day after day, but he kept doing it.

The point is, you have to find that thing—that reason—within yourself. No one can help you find that. Nothing outside of you can help you find that, and certainly there's yet to be a book written that can either. It's on you.

Do you have what it takes to master the game within your own heart and mind? If you do, then nothing—and no one—can stop you . . . and in order to get there, I just want you to know that it's okay to kiss that ass.